D0343584

staying strong

staying strong

365 days a year

Demi Lovato

headline

First published in the UK in 2013
by HEADLINE PUBLISHING GROUP

10

Cataloguing in Publication Data is available from the British Library

Book design by April Ward

Quotes for January 12, January 26, February 2 and August 20 © The Walt Disney Company

Hardback ISBN 978 1 4722 1807 0

Printed and bound in Great Britain by Clays Ltd, St Ives plc

Headline's policy is to use papers that are natural, renewable and recyclable products and made
from wood grown in sustainable forests. The logging and manufacturing processes are expected to
conform to the environmental regulations of the country of origin.

HEADLINE PUBLISHING GROUP
An Hachette UK Company
338 Euston Road
London NW1 3BH

www.headline.co.uk
www.hachette.co.uk

For my fans.

An introduction from

KATIE COURIC

I first met Demi over breakfast at the London Hotel in the summer of 2012. Her career was on fire. She had a huge hit in "Skyscraper," "Give Your Heart a Break" was climbing the charts (it would eventually hit #1), and she was months away from being named a judge on *The X Factor* alongside Simon Cowell and Britney Spears.

For a girl who had just turned 20 and made her name as a Disney teen queen, she seemed wise beyond her years. But she encountered more than a few bumps on her road to success. Demi shared her personal struggles with me, including her battles with anorexia and bulimia, bullying, self-harm and bipolar disorder, and how these challenges almost derailed her career.

As a mother of two daughters, I was so grateful that Demi was using her painful experiences to talk frankly to girls and let them know that fame doesn't necessarily shield you from insecurity and self-doubt. By pulling back the glossy curtain of celebrity and exposing her all-too-human side, I know Demi made countless young women with some of those same problems feel much less alone.

Not long after our first meeting, I welcomed Demi to the set of my daytime talk show. No surprise, she was charismatic and generous. Her willingness to speak so openly in a public forum inspired me to share my own experience with an eating disorder in my twenties, something that I had never spoken about before. Demi's honesty made me feel safe to be honest about my own past.

Demi has a unique relationship with her fans. They love her and she loves them right back. She's taught us all that we need to give our hearts a break at the low moments, and take the time to enjoy the view from the skyscraper when we hit our highs.

Whether you're 16, or, in my case, 56, you'll learn something from Demi's journey and life advice, and end up loving her even more.

staying strong

Dear Reader,

I have been through all kinds of experiences in my life, and I have faced struggles ranging from addiction to depression, all the while on a search for self-discovery and happiness. There are always going to be highs and lows, heartbreaks and victories, and everything in between. So sometimes the smallest few words can make all the difference; they can comfort and they can inspire.

Each day I meditate and pray by getting in touch with the higher power within me. No matter how old you are, where you come from, your race or religion, it is vital to have a higher power—something bigger than yourself that you can turn to for comfort. For me, it's God, but for you, it can be anything you believe in, the universe, karma, etc. Though some days can be a struggle, it's important to have something that will motivate, inspire, and help us stay positive and keep moving forward.

This book is a collection of my own words, quotes that inspire me, as well as lessons, meditations, reflections, and daily goals. They have helped me tremendously, and it's a special and personal gift that I want to share with all of you.

Wherever you are in life, please read these and know that I'm always there for you. Stay strong, be brave, love hard and true, and you will have nothing to lose.

All my love,

Demi

January

January 1

You are beautifully and wonderfully made.

A while back I decided I needed a mantra of my own. Something that was personal and meaningful that I could tell myself to bring comfort and love as well as root myself in the present moment. The Bible says "you are fearfully and wonderfully made," so I came up with "you are beautifully and wonderfully made." I say it to myself all the time, and it really helps me find peace knowing that I am perfect just as I am and that I don't need anything beyond what I have within me.

Goal: In this new year, come up with a mantra that is just yours. Each day, look in the mirror and repeat it back to yourself.

January 2

One's destination is never a place, but a new way of seeing things.

——HENRY MILLER

I've been so blessed to be able to travel so much over these last few years. One of the most profound things I witnessed while traveling was seeing how much we take for granted. I've seen slums where people are walking around without shoes or jackets in the freezing cold. I've been to places where people are working so hard at such physically demanding jobs while making hardly any money. It taught me to value every person on this planet and to not take my job for granted.

Goal: Stay open to anything and take a day (or week) seeing a new part of the world. If you can't afford to take time off work then visit a new neighborhood in your own town. Be grateful for everything you have.

Every life has a purpose. Share your story and you may help someone find their own.

The reason I decided to become honest about my personal struggles is because the issues that I've dealt with are still taboo to talk about. Self-harm, eating disorders, addiction, and mood disorders are things people aren't always open about. But it's so important that someone starts talking about these issues, so that those who are struggling know that there is help out there. It is my job to be a beacon of hope for the little girl that doesn't have any.

Goal: Stand up for those who can't yet. Give them support and strength.

Life can be so difficult at times, but fighting through the pain is so worth it. It's better to feel every kind of emotion than not feel at all.

I thought of this quote when I was at my dad's funeral and it's what got me through the experience. I was on such a roller coaster of emotions. In the past I would drink or restrict or find any way possible to avoid the immense pain I was in. People often choose to numb their pain with substances, but it's more courageous to walk through the fire with your eyes open. Instead of numbing my pain by using, I let myself feel all of the emotions that came to me. It was a difficult time in my life, but allowing myself to feel sadness and despair helped give way for the celebration of his life. It allowed me to begin healing in a healthy and honest fashion.

Goal: Allow yourself to feel the one thing you've been pushing away. Call a friend, be vulnerable, and share it with them.

There are so many beautiful, talented souls in this world. Don't let anything stand in the way of your potential.

I've encountered so many people in my life who tell me that I can't do something. Those people are just testing you and you can't let them bring you down. True friends will lift you up and believe in you. Don't allow anyone to tell you you can't live your dream because if you don't believe in yourself then nobody else will.

Goal: Think about one thing you've been holding back on doing and start doing it today. Be fearless.

January 6

Expose yourself to your deepest fear;
after that, fear has no power.

—JIM MORRISON

When I was a kid, I had the biggest fear of throwing up and then I ended up becoming bulimic. Subconsciously, I was acting out my greatest fear. I hated throwing up so much that I brought it upon myself.

Goal: Make sure you aren't living out your fears, but releasing them. Try to remember that there is a purpose for every hardship or opportunity in your life.

January 7

Change your thoughts, change your life.

—LAO TZU

When I was fighting depression, I remember hearing this expression and not understanding it at first. When I decided to implement it in my life, a whole new world opened up for me. Change the negative, self-loathing thoughts to positive, self-affirming ones. When you're positive about yourself and everything around you, you begin to see the world in a different light. Your life today is what *you* make of it.

Goal: Be mindful of the tone of your thoughts.

January 8

Love is the answer.

—ENGLAND DAN AND JOHN FORD COLEY

This simple lyric holds so much truth. Above all else, love makes everything right. There have been so many times in life when I felt lost and hopeless, but when I come back to the love I have in my heart for my friends and family and for my own life, I feel at peace.

Goal: Let everyone you love know it. Shout it from the rooftops, bake them a cake, write them a letter, or draw them a picture. Don't let them take your love for granted when you have so much to give.

January 9

Go where you are wanted and stray from where you aren't. Surround yourself with positive people and environments.

Don't waste time with people who don't appreciate and value you for everything you have to offer. I know so many girls who keep chasing guys thinking they can change them or friends who don't have their best interests at heart, but it doesn't work that way. One of the keys to lasting relationships and friendships is mutual respect.

Goal: Don't squander your time chasing anyone who has told you they don't want you around. Evaluate all your relationships and weed out the negative ones.

January 10

Don't invalidate your feelings.
Honor them.

I used to run and hide from my feelings especially when I felt something that was upsetting, painful, or uncomfortable. But over time I've learned to accept all of my feelings. I know that in order for me to work through them, I must first honor and embrace all emotions. They are a part of me. Therefore they are meaningful and valid.

Goal: Pick a feeling that you're afraid or ashamed of. Feeling fear, anger, or sadness is okay as long as you don't let it define you. Embrace your emotions and remind yourself how valuable they are.

January 11

You can steer yourself any direction you choose.

—DR. SEUSS

This is your life—you have everything you need inside you to live the life you have always dreamed of. Take all that you have learned and experienced and create your own reality. The beautiful part about life is that if you don't like where you are, there's always a new moment and a new day to start again.

Goal: Make smart, educated decisions. Encourage yourself to make the choices today for the future you want tomorrow.

January 12

A dream is a wish your heart makes.

—*Cinderella*

As simple as this sounds, it's one of the most profound messages that any of the Disney fairy tales have given us. We can grow up being whoever we want to be—wherever we want to be. If you have a goal, try to go after it with all your heart. Anything is possible.

Goal: Make a wish with all your heart and chase every dream you have. Only you can reach your goals. No one else can achieve them for you.

January 13

Become your own best friend.

Over the years I have had to learn to become my own best friend. There were many nights I spent crying myself to sleep, sad and lonely with almost every given heartache. Over time I realized that I had to learn to comfort myself to overcome the pain. It's a process, and I'm still learning how to do it, but I've gotten so much better. I can honestly say that I am my own best friend.

Goal: Love yourself and treat yourself as you would treat your very best friend. You deserve the same love you give to others.

It matters not what someone is born, but what they grow to be.

—J. K. ROWLING

Each and every one of us has a different beginning to our story. Our lives all start in different places, but when we dedicate our hearts and minds to what we are most passionate about, there is no stopping us. Reward and success are measured by how much you try and how much you receive.

Goal: Be proud of who you are and where you came from. Look forward to wherever it is you are going and who it is you want to be.

January 15

My mama always used to tell me
if you can't find something to live for,
you best find something to die for.

—TUPAC

Each of us has a purpose on this beautiful earth. What we make of our lives and how we choose to fulfill it is up to us. What is most important is that you have a cause, something you believe in that lights up your life and connects you to your life's purpose.

Goal: Find something in life that makes you get up in the morning, and keep on doing that. Stand up for the things you believe in.

When your feet start to hurt, place yourself in someone else's shoes.

It's so easy to get caught up in your own world and let dramas consume you. It's usually difficult to even realize you're doing it because you're so deep in it. This can be dangerous because you can quickly lose touch with reality. Don't invalidate your emotions or hardships, but remember that someone out there has it worse.

Goal: Get some perspective by doing community service or charity work. Make a list of 10–15 things or people you're grateful for—no matter how simple or important they may seem.

January 17

Remember, no one can make you feel inferior without your consent.

——ELEANOR ROOSEVELT

There are people in this life who will take advantage of you and tell you who they think you are. It's up to you what you do with that information. The moment you let people make decisions on your behalf you have given up your dignity. But you can always get it back as long as you remember to connect with your higher power.

Goal: Don't let anyone take advantage or manipulate you. Remind yourself that you're entitled to the life and love you deserve.

January 18

I'm a firm believer that everything happens for a reason.

I don't believe in coincidences. I think that things happen the way that they are supposed to. When you really look at and evaluate every experience you've had, it's a direct result of your actions and thoughts.

Goal: Don't fight or wish away unexpected occurrences. In time, and in its own way, it will prove to better your life in some way.

The most common way people give up their power is by thinking they don't have any.

—ALICE WALKER

When you let people tear you down and say you have nothing to offer, you are giving in to them. You're basically giving them permission by way of submission. Nobody has the right to take your power away—it is yours and yours alone.

Goal: Use the voice that you were given. Shout what you believe in from the top of your lungs. Never let anyone quiet you.

January 20

Nobody but you knows what is right for you, so listen to your instincts.

Listen to that little voice inside yourself, like a loving parent or a good friend. This is the truest part of your soul, the key to your happiness. Sometimes thoughts, fears, or other people get too loud and we can't hear ourselves. Do what you need to do to get back in touch.

Goal: Today, follow what your heart tells you.

Worry does not empty tomorrow of its sorrow; it empties today of its strength.

—CORRIE TEN BOOM

I think sometimes people believe that worrying has some kind of productive purpose. Worry sucks all of your energy and joy out of whatever it is you're doing. It's human nature to worry, but when we do it constantly, we run into more problems. It may give you something to do, but you don't get anywhere.

Goal: The next time you are worrying about something, try to remember that you aren't always in control. Instead, do practical things like make a budget or create a schedule. Be proactive and let go of the stress. After all, it won't change a thing.

Never be ashamed of what you feel.
You have the right to feel any
emotion that you want and to
do what makes you happy.

We aren't robots. What makes us exceptional as human beings is that we have the capacity to feel so many emotions all at once. Even though that can sometimes be overwhelming it's still pretty amazing what our bodies can do. Sometimes I've laughed from crying or cried from laughing. Either way, emotions aren't a sign of weakness, but a sign of strength and passion.

Goal: Watch a movie that makes you laugh or listen to a song that makes you cry. Embrace your emotions and be proud of what you feel.

January 23

Imperfection is beauty, madness is
genius, and it's better to be absolutely
ridiculous than absolutely boring.

——MARILYN MONROE

I never found out until I went into treatment that I was bipolar. It was there that I learned that bipolar disorder is a mental illness. It's not anything that I can control, which is why I had to get help for it, and for that I'm not ashamed. Everyone is carrying a full wagon, whether it's as simple as a pimple or as severe as mental illness, but when you remember that each of us has our own struggles, you realize that we must come together to help support each other.

Goal: No matter how little a problem may seem, be kind and find support for what you or a friend is dealing with. Look at page 399 for some resources to help.

January 24

Our secrets make us sick.

—UNKNOWN

Our secrets can be so toxic and we don't even realize it. I had to learn that keeping things inside me was part of why I wanted to use alcohol and drugs in the first place—to hide from myself. When I started opening up, I started to heal. By talking to someone and expressing how I feel, I'm able to relieve the power of the emotion that's been weighing me down.

Goal: Share something you've been hiding with a close friend or family member. See how much better you feel afterward.

January 25

Strive not to be a success,
but rather to be of value.

—ALBERT EINSTEIN

It's so easy to get caught up in wanting success, wealth, and fame. If that's the kind of recognition you seek in life, it won't last because it's not authentic. We are here to be of service, to be of value, and to help others in our own unique ways. Success doesn't define who we are. It's only a reminder of what we can achieve.

Goal: Think about what matters to you and make sure you are doing things for the right reasons and not to please your ego. Make sure your intentions are healthy for you.

January 26

Just do your best and take a rest and sing yourself a song.

—*Snow White*

Sometimes there's nothing else you can do but your best. Take the time you need for you and find something that brings you joy. For me it's singing. When I sing or play music I'm able to relieve myself of whatever I'm struggling with. If your passion is playing sports, get outside and play! If you're working too hard, try some meditation or yoga. The important thing is to take care of ourselves.

Goal: Sing out loud today. Make yourself laugh or dance like a fool. Treat yourself to whatever makes you happy. You deserve it!

January 27

Learn from the past and share your experiences with others. Cherish the present and look forward to the future.

There's a difference between hanging on to the past and learning from it. What's done is done, and I realized it's important not to dwell because I can't change what's already happened. But at the same time I want to be mindful of the past and learn from my mistakes and my successes in life. The future excites me too, but at the end of the day, all we have is this moment now and we must cherish and love it.

Goal: Make a conscious effort to live in the present today. When you catch yourself obsessing over the past or worrying about the future just remember you are exactly where you need to be right now.

January 28

I want to grow old without face-lifts.
I want to have the courage to be loyal
to the face I have made.

—MARILYN MONROE

It's not always easy to feel perfectly comfortable and proud of the skin we are living in. We have days where our skin is bad, our hair isn't right, we feel fat, and we can't find an outfit to make it all work. Every single person feels this way from time to time. It takes courage to love yourself just as you are.

Goal: Discover how refreshing it is to not criticize yourself. Instead of criticizing your body parts, remind yourself how blessed you are to have them.

January 29

Religious people are afraid of going to hell,
but spiritual people are the ones who have
been to hell and don't want to go back.

—ANONYMOUS

Walking around on eggshells trying not to offend people is a
waste of time. It's easy to get caught up in trying to please others
that it takes away from being ourselves. You aren't going to be
perfect or loved by everyone. It's so much more gratifying and
purposeful to just live your life and learn from your mistakes so
that you don't have to go through them again.

Goal: Be who you are and don't allow anyone to affect the
confidence you have in your individuality.

January 30

Sticks and stones may break her bones
but words and names can make her
wanna kill herself.

—UNKNOWN

People say sticks and stones may break your bones, but names can never hurt you—but that's so far from the truth. Sometimes words impact us more than physical pain. Things from the past were said to me that hurt me to this day. I remember saying to my mom how I would much rather have had the bullies hit me or punch me than say the cruel things they said, because the things they said changed my life forever.

Goal: Stand up for someone who is getting bullied in school or at work. Remind yourself and others of just how powerful words can really be. And when you're talking to others, choose your words wisely.

January 31

Every dream begins with a dreamer.
Always remember, you have within you
the strength, the patience, and the passion
to reach for the stars to change the world.

—HARRIET TUBMAN

We all have to start somewhere and we must remember that our journeys aren't mapped out for us. Dreams and visions will evolve and change as you do.

Goal: Be a fearless dreamer—the world is your oyster. Write down the top 5–10 things you want to accomplish in the next month. Never stop striving to be the best you can be!

February

When we show our love,
the world opens its arms for us.

You get back what you put out in the world. Put out positive energy and positivity is what you will receive. It's amazing how love can calm any situation. Even if other people behave in ways that are toxic or harmful, when you respond with love and compassion, it is powerful. Whatever the result is, you know you can sleep at night knowing you've done right, and that's all you can control.

Goal: Wear your heart on your sleeve today and let the world know how much love you have inside you. Hug as many people or make as many people smile as you can.

If your heart is in your dream, no request is too extreme.

—Pinocchio

All that matters is that you follow and pursue what you love. As long as you are honoring your truest desires there's no dream too big. In fact the bigger you allow yourself to dream, the more joy you invite into your life.

Goal: Allow yourself to have the biggest dreams today, and find peace knowing that simply by dreaming about them you are one step closer to realizing them.

February 3

My only advice is to stay aware, listen carefully, and yell for help if you need it.

—JUDY BLUME

Keep evolving, keep growing, keep making mistakes, fall in love, get your heart broken, grow from it, and do it again. Everything we go through allows us to become more alive, more vibrant, and more joyous. Don't let fear or shame bring you down. Keep going, keep living.

Goal: Confront one of your fears today. Try to remember something difficult you went through and what you learned from it. How did it make you stronger?

February 4

A problem is never solved without a solution.
Better sooner than later!

I try to start every day by doing the things I'm most anxious about because it makes me feel stronger and more empowered as I go about my day. When our worries or anxieties are silenced, we are free to move on to better things.

Goal: Take care of all your outstanding loose ends today—no matter what. I guarantee that you will feel so much lighter today and possibly for the rest of the week.

February 5

Weeping may endure for a night
but joy cometh in the morning.

—PSALM 30:5

Sometimes we need tears to be able to access the deepest joy. When times are hard, make sure you allow yourself to feel the sadness. Let your tears fall knowing that they will surely pass and something wonderful is on its way to you.

Goal: If you're sad, take some time to try and remember the joy that will undoubtedly follow. Remember it's always darkest before the dawn.

I think scars are like battle wounds—
beautiful in a way. They show what
you've been through and how strong
you are for coming out of it.

A scar is a symbol of having experienced something profound. Some of us have physical scars that we can see; when we look at them, they remind us of a trying journey we went through. For many of us the scars are invisible—they are metaphors for a battle we fought and overcame.

Goal: Reflect on your scars and how they helped shape your life for the better.

February 7

When you learn how to communicate with others, there is almost no problem you cannot solve together.

People will always disagree because no two people are alike. Each of us comes with our own complex history, which informs how we see ourselves and the world around us. I used to get overwhelmed and frustrated when I didn't feel like I could get on the same page with someone. But I've realized over time that what's vital to human relationships isn't agreeing on everything— it's learning how to talk through our disagreements.

Goal: Lovingly confront a friend or colleague if something has been on your mind. Don't hide things that upset you, but calmly try to figure out a way you can collectively fix the issues. Express how the problem makes you *feel* and a way you can prevent it from reoccurring.

Only those who will risk going too far can possibly find out how far one can go.

—T. S. ELIOT

We learn by trying, by pushing the envelope fearlessly with conviction. It's better to try and fail than to imagine what would have happened. The what-if's can be debilitating.

Goal: Don't hold back on what matters to you—see how much of yourself you can give; see how far you can go. Try your hardest to have the life you want today so you never have future regrets. What can you do today to create the life you want tomorrow?

February 9

The greatest wealth is health.

—ROMAN POET

Good health is something all the riches in the world can't buy. Take good care of yourself and count your blessings. Be thankful you woke up today because not every day is guaranteed. I spent so long taking my God-given health for granted that I forgot how blessed I am to be alive today. Our body is our temple. Treat it like your sanctuary.

Goal: Do something good for your body today. Go for a run or a hike or take a yoga class. But most importantly, be grateful for the life you're living today.

Do not go where the path may lead, go instead where there is no path and leave a trail.

—RALPH WALDO EMERSON

Sometimes it's easier and safer to follow others. But if we never sought out new landscapes or ideas we would never have any of the wonderful innovations we have today. Had Thomas Edison never believed in electricity, we would not have light. If Rosa Parks hadn't stood up for what she believed in, she wouldn't have inspired others to do the same. We have the ability to change the world if we refuse to listen to the voice that says, "we can't" or "we shouldn't."

Goal: Break out and start your own path—innovate. Think outside the box. Anything is possible.

February 11

The emotion that can break your heart is sometimes the very one that heals it.

—NICHOLAS SPARKS

Oftentimes, when I'm struggling with loss or heartbreak, I waste so much time looking for answers that I had within myself all along. I get a million opinions on how to deal with something or someone, but I overlook the most obvious part, which is that the same thing that is causing pain also has the power to heal me.

Goal: Remember that there isn't always an immediate solution. Be patient and ask for help and guidance from someone with more life experience.

See the inner child in everyone.

Sometimes when I'm getting frustrated or annoyed with someone, I remember that they were once a child.

I close my eyes and I visualize how they must have been when they were little and when I reopen my eyes, all I can feel for that person is love and compassion. Whatever happened to them to make them act the way they are no longer matters; it's their innocence that prevails, and I have no choice but to be humbled in their presence.

Goal: See the potential for good in everyone and have compassion for your foes. Remember that you never know what happens behind closed doors. Therefore, have mercy on their actions. It's likely that they're in pain themselves.

February 13

Don't wait, the time will never be just right.

—NAPOLEON HILL

Sometimes we wait for exactly the right moment to do something. I've found that this whole waiting thing can delay our happiness. Most of the major moments in my life occurred because I pursued them. It doesn't mean that sometimes something wonderful won't just magically happen because it will, especially if you're doing the work and thinking positively. But sometimes in life we have to just go for it and take a risk.

Goal: Take your first big step toward something you keep telling yourself to wait on.

Wherever you go, go with all your heart.

——CONFUCIUS

As long as we let our hearts lead us we will always make honest and authentic choices that we can stand by. I believe our world needs more people who lead with their hearts and give love without question or demands. If we all act on things we are passionate about, we have a stronger chance to achieve our goals.

Goal: Listen to your intuitions and remember your gut doesn't lie. Trust your soul and spread love to others.

February 15

Never getting help doesn't make you brave.

——STRAYLIGHT RUN, "SYMPATHY FOR THE MARTYR"

When the stress of holding heavy emotions in piles up, it can do more damage than you will ever realize. It's never easy to ask for help, but please find it in yourself to do so. Write a note, call someone, do whatever is needed to send an SOS. Help is always waiting and the bravest people in the world are those who can ask for it.

Goal: Be brave and tell someone you need help.

February 16

If you have good thoughts, they will
shine out of your face like sunbeams,
and you will always look lovely.

—ROALD DAHL

When you are in control of your life and your happiness, your joy is infectious. Nothing in this world makes a person look more beautiful than when they are beaming with happiness. You never know how a simple smile or "how are you, really?" to a friend could change their day, or even, life.

Goal: Smile and show the world how beautiful you are. Be conscious of people's emotions around you and remember the impact you can have on them.

February 17

I'm selfish, impatient, and a little insecure.
I make mistakes, I'm out of control, and at
times hard to handle. But if you can't handle
me at my worst, then you sure as hell
don't deserve me at my best.

—MARILYN MONROE

Anybody who really loves and supports you will always be there for you. The best way to find out who your real friends are is to see who sticks around in your times of turmoil and suffering. If they can't accept you when you're struggling then they most certainly don't deserve you at your best. It's so important to keep that in mind when it comes to making decisions about who to surround yourself with.

Goal: Make sure you're being the sort of friend that you'd want in your own life. Be grateful for those relationships that prove they deserve you.

February 18

Confidence starts with beauty.
Beauty begins from comfort within.

I've been to parties where I've seen these really gorgeous girls hiding in the corners afraid to talk to anyone. I can tell they're insecure. Maybe they don't think they're pretty enough or they don't think they have the right outfit on, but it immediately dims their inner light. To me there's nothing more attractive than someone owning who they are in the skin they're in.

Goal: Find what makes you comfortable and confident. Remember how special you are and wear it with pride!

February 19

Mistakes are nothing more than opportunities to learn, grow, and better our future.

It's so easy to beat ourselves up for mistakes we've made in the past. Mistakes are part of being human and they are part of being alive. Our mistakes are blessings and opportunities to keep learning and expanding. But even when you learn from your mistakes don't expect to never make another. You will and that's okay.

Goal: Keep growing and embrace each challenge as a chance to learn something new and you will be amazed by how easy it is to move on.

I know it's an experience that I need to have
if God's putting me through it.

—LIL WAYNE

Sometimes when things are really trying and painful all we can think is, why on earth do I have to go through this, why do I deserve this? But there's a better way to approach a trying moment in life. Instead of resisting it, try surrendering to it and considering that there's a reason it has been given to you and not somebody else. If you are dealing with it, it is part of your journey.

Goal: The next time you go through a trying time, find the ways in which you can grow and learn instead of dwelling on your suffering.

When people don't express themselves, they die one piece at a time.

—LAURIE HALSE ANDERSON

Music has always helped me express what I cannot say with words. One of the most rewarding things about my profession is that I get to use my voice and my songs to help touch others and give them strength. I know exactly what it is like to sit alone in your room, broken down, bruised inside and out, lonely, and desperate to feel loved and connected to someone. My songs are not only for me, but they are for every single person out there in need of a friend. They are for anyone who has ever felt like they needed someone to stand by their side. If you are reading this book, please know I am here for you, and I want to be there to help you get through your darkest days.

Goal: Put on any song that always makes you feel better. If you're a musician/songwriter then pick up your instrument and express yourself.

February 22

The best and most beautiful things in the world cannot be seen or even touched —they must be felt with the heart.

—HELEN KELLER

It is the intangible things that make life so amazing. The most incredible memories in my life have been experiences and emotions that can't be described or re-created. I spent so many years trying to create a high from drugs and alcohol when little did I know, the strongest high had been right in front of me the entire time—life.

Goal: Take the time to slow down and experience something you cannot see but something beautiful that you can feel.

February 23

Always be a first-rate version of
yourself instead of a second-rate
version of someone else.

—JUDY GARLAND

Just like snowflakes, there is no one else on this planet like you.
Don't waste your time trying to be like other people. Be the best
you and own it. You're best at being yourself—not anyone else.
If we all looked, talked, and walked the same, no one would be
unique. Individuality wouldn't exist. Being different is what
makes us special and the world so exciting.

Goal: Assess your character. Be certain that you're not
modeling yourself after someone, but just being who you are
meant to be. Go ahead, be weird because "normal" is boring!

February 24

Courage to change.

—UNKNOWN

Change is part of life but for some reason, it can feel scary. Change means growth and growth means that we're evolving. I remember when I was a kid, my parents told me I had to learn certain lessons in order to grow up. As I got older I realized my lessons not only became more difficult to understand and overcome, but they also became more valuable. It's made my life much more meaningful. Growing takes courage, so as you go through your own growing pains in life just remember to stay strong and be brave and courageous, because you are growing and becoming a better person.

Goal: What's something you'd like to change about your life or yourself? Find the courage to start making it happen one step at a time.

February 25

No matter what you have been
through in life, good or bad, don't take
it for granted. There are lessons in
every moment of our lives.

Each of us leads unique lives with experiences that nobody else
will ever completely understand. Your story holds so many
valuable lessons that can help inspire, teach, and motivate
someone else should you choose to share it. In treatment, I heard
so many different stories. Just by listening, I learned so many
different things. I'm so thankful I found the courage to share my
story and talk about what I've been through. Not only has it
helped me, but it's helped give perspective and strength to so
many other people. I encourage you to do the same.

Goal: Share your story with someone. You never know how
one sentence of your life story could inspire someone to rewrite
their own.

Nothing is impossible; the word itself says "I'm possible."

—AUDREY HEPBURN

What is possible in this life is relative to what you're capable of. As we expand our knowledge and consciousness, we continue to grow, and the things that we thought were not possible suddenly become attainable. The more we are encouraged to expand our knowledge and our perceptions about how things work in our lives, the more we are able to accomplish.

Goal: Put your mind to a chore or task today. Turn impossible into possible. Make a list of ways your biggest dreams can one day come true.

For to set the mind on the flesh is death, for to set the mind on the Spirit is life and peace.

—ROMANS 8:6

As someone who has dealt with an eating disorder most of my life, I have spent so much time focusing on what was on the outside rather than what was on the inside. In a way I was dead on the inside. When I started focusing on myself, who I really was, I started to cultivate a loving relationship with myself. It was only then that I was able to feel confident and beautiful in my own skin.

Goal: Focus on what you have inside that makes you beautiful. List 5–10 nonphysical attributes of yourself that make you the spectacular human being that you truly are.

February 28

People need people—
we're all in this together.

When we are hiding from ourselves, it's so easy to become isolated. Over time, we start internalizing our emotions, engaging reclusive behavior, and before we know it, we're completely alone. This can leave us feeling depressed. While it's vital to know how to be alone and comfortable with yourself, we also must remember that we need the love and companionship of others. When I stopped isolating myself and reconnected with friends and family, I felt a weight fall off my shoulders.

Goal: Reach out to those closest to you and begin rebuilding those relationships. Step out of your comfort zone and think of ways you can seek support from others.

March

Sometimes the greatest gift you can give yourself is a gift you give to someone else.

When I was thirteen years old, I gave $150 of babysitting money to my church. I was so proud of myself for performing this good deed that I had to go tell every single person I knew. Later that day I didn't feel as good about my kind act and I couldn't figure out why. I realized that I was doing it partly for the recognition, not just from a good place in my heart. It's important to do good things for other people without expecting anything in return. The pure and simple gesture of compassion speaks volumes and helps others and ourselves in ways we can't even fully comprehend.

Goal: Perform a loving act of kindness anonymously. Do something today for a stranger expecting nothing in return and cherish the feeling you get from giving.

March 2

Hate is only a form of love that hasn't found a way to express itself logically.

—LIL WAYNE

In school, I felt hatred toward my bullies. I realized that resenting others was only hurting myself. I ended up projecting my insecurities and taking it out on other people. A chain reaction. If I had been more resolved and confident in my ability to love myself, I would have found more productive ways to confront and rise above the negativity around me.

Goal: Don't let hate get the best of you. Have compassion for your bullies today by understanding their actions are only a result of unhappiness and pain within themselves.

The question isn't who is going to let me; it's who is going to stop me.

—AYN RAND

If I'd believed all the people who told me that I didn't have what it takes to make it, I would be nowhere. It took me a while to build up my confidence. It can be really scary, but it's better to rise to the challenge and overcome those feelings because in the end those people don't matter. Along my journey I stopped worrying about all the nonsense. I gave up trying to control my destiny and let the love of what I do best take over instead of worrying about failure. The only one who was actually stopping me was myself. Whenever I encounter people now who tell me I can't achieve something, it just reminds me that I shouldn't listen to them. But only believe in myself.

Goal: Is there someone in your life who keeps trying to get in the way of your success? It might be time to have a talk with them or let them out of your life.

Trust is a bond between two people that is found only when they are able to listen and understand where the other person is coming from. That to me is the key to friendships and relationships.

Relationships between family, friends, significant others, and colleagues are complicated and full of learning experiences. Nobody comes into this world knowing everything. We all go through different experiences, make mistakes, have successes, and then make more mistakes that we can learn from. The ability to trust and listen to the people in your life is the foundation all healthy relationships are built on.

Goal: When talking to friends, make sure you are really listening to what they have to say and aren't distracted by something else. You owe that to them and you would want the same in return.

March 5

From now on we live in a world where
man has walked on the moon. It's not
a miracle, we just decided to go.

—JIM LOVELL

Most things that we dream about are actually achievable. When we look up at the sky and see the moon so far away, it seems impossible and unfathomable that a human being has actually been up there. But mankind made it happen and it all started with a dream.

Goal: Believe in the impossible today. It may not be impossible after all. What's your dream?

March 6

Cherish the moment.

This moment right here, while you're reading this book, is all you have. You have yourself and your life today, which is all you ever need. We spend so much time focusing on the past or our future that we forget how blessed we are to still be here surrounded by beautiful things.

Goal: Try to live in the moment. Appreciate the life you are living right now and how blessed you are to still be alive today.

March 7

I'm grateful for all the love and all the
heartache I've experienced in my life.
Both have been equally wonderful.

In love I have been elated and brokenhearted and felt every emotion in between. As I've gotten older I've learned to embrace the
painful parts, because I realize they make me stronger and they
are just parts of life. It hurts to power through the rough times
but just like a muscle, it must be exercised before it's able to
become stronger.

Goal: Think about a specific painful moment in your life, and
then think about how that feeling didn't last forever even though
you thought it would. Remember that life will continue to go on
and time really does heal all wounds.

March 8

The only way to have a friend is to be one.

—RALPH WALDO EMERSON

You can't expect others to treat you well unless you yourself treat people well. Sometimes you can't really know how to be a good friend until you need one. The golden rule is something we've all heard a million times growing up—treat other people the way you want to be treated. It may seem cliché but if more people lived by that motto, the world would be a much better place.

Goal: Think about something you wish one of your friends would do for you and do it for them. Pay attention to the way you interact with others.

March 9

All of our actions have consequences. What we do will eventually come back to us, which is why it's always best to act with kindness.

—YEHUDA BERG

It is so important to be thoughtful and considerate about what we do and how we treat others. You can't tiptoe around other people, but you also have to treat people with genuine kindness and respect. When you act out of jealousy or negativity, you have to be prepared for the consequences of your actions.

Goal: Try to make at least fifteen people smile today. It's actually a really fun game to play with a friend to see who can get to fifteen first. You never know when those people will smile back when you need it most.

If something doesn't feel right, trust your instincts. It's better to be safe than sorry.

So often in life we find ourselves in situations where we are desperately trying to figure out how we got there in the first place. Before we know it, we are in so deep that there's a strange sense of obligation to follow through with it. If something feels wrong to you, you shouldn't do it. If your friends try to pressure you into doing something you don't feel like doing, or if your boss/coworker insists you make an unethical decision, question their intention and your own. Only do what feels right to *you*.

Goal: Do only what makes you feel comfortable because you are your only guide.

If I'm going to sing like someone else, then I don't need to sing at all.

—BILLIE HOLIDAY

You have to live your life as you. When someone asks you to be like someone else, it's important to know yourself well enough to stay true to who you are. Confidence and fearlessness of what others think about you are the most attractive qualities. After all, when you try to be someone you're not, most of the time, people can see right through it.

Goal: Sing your own song; dance your own dance. You don't need to imitate or be like anyone else.

March 12

There is a crack, a crack in everything,
that's how the light gets in.

—LEONARD COHEN, "ANTHEM"

So much beauty and joy in my life has come from going through something really difficult. When I emerge from the darkness, I am able to appreciate that it's over. The pain has made me grow and evolve into something better, stronger, and filled with more gratitude for all that my life has to offer. The light at the end of the tunnel can seem miles and miles away, but the more faith you have, the sooner you'll find it.

Goal: Find hope in a dark situation.

Don't be afraid to stand up for what you
believe in even if it means standing alone.

—UNKNOWN

There are times in life when it feels like you are the only one who
sees things a certain way. As long as you are always following
your heart and your conscience and honoring what feels right, it
doesn't really matter what other people think. You must stand
your ground and do the right thing. Throughout history, movements defending civil rights started with just a few people.
Everyone was against them and ridiculed them, but they stood
their ground. In the end those movements changed history and
paved the way for so many incredible people to be treated with
dignity and equality.

Goal: Stand up for something or someone today. It could be a
stranger or someone you love. Or join forces with a team of
people standing up for what you believe in.

Honor every feeling and you can live truthfully.

One of the things I've come to love about life is that it's never just one thing. At times we are filled with joy, boredom, or loss and despair. All of these emotions make up the fabric of our lives. We cannot control everything, but we can control how we allow these varied moments to affect us. I used to take every disappointment as a major loss, a personal statement about the future of dreams. Now I have learned that life will be filled with every shade of feeling, every texture of emotion, and that there's beauty in that as long as I honor myself truthfully in every moment.

Goal: Think about someone or something that broke your heart and then think about how that made you change and grow for the better.

March 15

God, grant me the serenity to accept
the things I cannot change,
The courage to change the things I can,
And wisdom to know the difference.

—REINHOLD NIEBUHR, "SERENITY PRAYER"

Today is the anniversary of my sobriety, so I wanted to share the serenity prayer. Those who are recovering use this prayer on a daily basis, but what is truly amazing about it is that you don't have to be in recovery to speak these words. I have spoken this prayer almost every day of my recovery and it has helped simplify the sea of emotions and feelings that often run through me, especially on a hard day. We do the best we can in life, we take things one day at a time, and sometimes we all just need a simple reminder of that.

Goal: Speak this prayer aloud to yourself or with a friend today and observe how it makes you feel. Repeat it daily for a week and allow it to change your perspective on things.

Find your inner light and let it light up the world.

Each one of us has something different to offer and contribute to this world. We're all just trying to figure out our lives and each of us does it differently. To me that kind of self-discovery is so fascinating. You have a light inside you and we need that light to be able to understand things more clearly. Don't let anyone dim your light because without it none of us can see.

Goal: Let your light shine. How can you be a light to others?

March 17

If you're spending your entire life chasing the next party, what are you running away from?

There are so many figures in popular music and culture who want people to think they are strong and tough because they use substances and party all night long. To me strong is when you can sit through your problems and feel your emotions, when you don't have to hide them. There have been nights where I've had to sit on my hands because I want to act out, because I physically can't sit still in the pain or I'm trying to distract myself from living in the moment.

Goal: Stop running and start dealing with life and your problems. It could be as simple as not checking your phone when you're uncomfortable or alone. Listen to what's going on in your mind and respect the thoughts coming to you.

March 18

Dream big or go home. As far as we know
we are here only once, so release your
fear and embrace your dreams.

Don't waste another second not doing what you love. Your
dreams are yours for a reason so run after them fearlessly with
open arms. Everything I've achieved in life came to me because
I knew what I wanted and I went for it wholeheartedly. Having
big dreams used to scare me, but once I started achieving them
I started embracing them, and that's when they started embracing me.

Goal: Write down every dream you have for your life.
Remember, no dream is too big for you. The world is yours for
the taking.

March 19

Don't make assumptions. Find the courage to ask questions and to express what you really want. Communicate with others as clearly as you can to avoid misunderstandings, sadness, and drama. With just this one agreement, you can completely transform your life.

—MIGUEL ANGEL RUIZ

It's better to take the time to ask questions and to find the words to say what you really feel. Often we leave so much room for interpretation either because we are rushing or because we are afraid to speak the whole truth, but this is where miscommunications start. So even if you aren't sure about what someone means or how they feel, just ask them.

Goal: When was the last time you assumed something and were wrong? Make a point to know the truth and not assume it.

You will always be tempted and tested to take the easy way out.

Our values are always going to be tested. We will always be tempted to take the easy way out, lie, cheat, and steal because sometimes those things seem easier, but I promise you that they have a way of catching up to you. I can't tell you how important it is to check yourself before you do something you regret. Don't succumb to pressure and don't let anyone influence your decisions or actions.

Goal: If you have a friend or colleague who lies, cheats, or steals, it's important to let them know that their values do not line up with yours, and when their bad habits start affecting you.

March 21

In every community, there is work to be done. In every nation, there are wounds to heal. In every heart is the power to do it.

——MARIANNE WILLIAMSON

For all the problems, disasters, and tragedies that we hear about daily, it's important to not let such sadness overwhelm and flood you with despair. Where there is dark there is also light. Sometimes the most beautiful rainbows come from the worst storms.

Goal: How can you spread love, hope, and faith to others today? Ask yourself if there's someone in particular in your life needing your support.

You can't resolve other people's issues, but you can sit with them and share the burden of their pain, thereby lightening it.

—YEHUDA BERG

Often when we're comforting loved ones, all that we want to do is take their pain away. It's such a natural desire to help those we love in need. But there are many times when it is necessary for people to go through pain to fully learn and emerge stronger than ever. Remember not to enable someone who needs help with a problem. Support them in finding a solution.

Goal: The next time a loved one is going through a difficult period, think about how you can support them instead of fixing them.

March 23

Never judge a book by its cover.

—UNKNOWN

It's so easy to walk by people and make judgments about who they are based on some small passing detail or flaw that you've observed. Maybe their attitude appears to be rude. Maybe they aren't as outgoing as you are. Either way, without taking the time to actually get to know someone and hear what they've been through, you really have no right to judge anyone. The things we observe superficially are just that; they are false impressions that don't tell you anything about what others have actually experienced.

Goal: Take the time to really get to know people, ask them what their story is, and be a good listener.

March 24

I believe that life is a prize, but to live doesn't mean you're alive.

—NICKI MINAJ, "MOMENT 4 LIFE"

Life is precious, and it's what you do with it that keeps you alive on the inside. It's not enough just to live and take that gift for granted. Each one of us has fears, but the more we work to overcome them, the more we are able to enjoy our lives. Fear varies by perspective or experience. When I was thirteen years old, I was in a severe car accident. My head gets clouded with all kinds of fears when I get in a car to this day. But the thing is, if you're living your life in fear, then you're just not living.

Goal: Try to face one of your fears today.

It is the mark of an educated mind to be able to entertain a thought without accepting it.

—ARISTOTLE

There is a lot of ignorance in our world. Ignorance leads to war, violence, hatred, judgement, intolerance, and unhappiness. No matter what your level of education, we all have the option and ability to seek more knowledge and gain understanding if we try. Even if you have beliefs different from someone else's, or if you argue because of a disagreement, we should all be more open to criticism and opinions.

Goal: Hear all sides and come to your own conclusions. Politely agree to disagree with someone if an argument or debate arises.

No matter how broken my heart may feel, I will always be grateful it still has a beat.

I've had a number of romantic heartaches in my twenty-one years. Relationships are fun, exciting, beautiful, and intriguing. But also complicated. I know that we all have heartbreaks in life, but now when they happen, I let myself feel the pain. Even though it hurts I remember that it was worth it because I was able to feel something so deeply. The fact that I could feel that kind of love and let someone into my heart means I'm alive and capable of so much.

Goal: Feel deep gratitude for all the people who have come into your life, positive and negative, because they've all taught you something.

Always remember there's a little girl inside you; treat her as if you just met her today.

It always amazes me how easily and readily we allow ourselves to self-loathe. We get in the habit of saying such terrible things to ourselves and we no longer realize how much damage we are doing. Would you say these things to your four-year-old self? Sometimes when I get really sick or tired while working, instead of taking care of myself, I force myself to push through it. I forget that there's a fragile little girl inside of me. Always ask that before you berate yourself, and refrain. How would you treat a child if they were sick? It's important to take care of yourself no matter what.

Goal: Treat yourself with kindness. Love the child inside of you and take care of him/her as if he/she was your own.

Why fit in when you're born to stand out?

—DR. SEUSS

Embrace all your eccentricities. We aren't made to blend in—we are all individuals. Sometimes we think we are supposed to hide our differences, but we shouldn't. It can be scary trying to figure out who you are and what your purpose is in life. But it's important to find the answer so you can accept and be who you really are.

Goal: Don't hide from yourself, let the world know who you really are and be proud of it.

There's not going to be a day when I don't think about food or my body, but I'm living with it and I wish I could tell young girls to find their safe place and stay with it.

Whether you are a man or woman, everyone deals with their insecurities, especially in a world where our looks are given so much value. Every day, people struggle, but somehow individually we each find it within ourselves to carry on and continue to stay strong. We aren't what we eat and our flaws do *not* define us.

Goal: Rise above society's superficial body-image standards. You are better than that and you deserve to just be who you are.

March 30

What you resist persists.

—CARL JUNG

If you find yourself spending too much time fearing something, you are bringing the energy and thoughts of that thing into your life rather than letting it go.

Goal: Have faith that you will be taken care of in this life, and don't dwell on or obsess about the rest.

March 31

Listen to other people's stories and find the strength and beauty in their actions.

I love to hear my fans' stories because they are so inspiring. They tell me how they have overcome bullying, eating disorders, addictions, cutting, and it's amazing how much strength we each have inside us. I also believe that when you share your story, the strength in you grows and the inspirational effect you have on others multiplies. It takes courage to open up to others.

Goal: Call a friend in need and tell them a story about when you had a hard time and how you got through it.

April

April 1

Doubt is a pain too lonely to know
that faith is his twin brother.

—KAHLIL GIBRAN

It may be April Fools' Day, but you are no fool, so stop doubting everything you do. Trust your instincts and believe in yourself enough to make the right decisions. We all have instincts for a reason.

Goal: When you find yourself doubting, stop it right there and say instead, "I believe in myself."

April 2

Sometimes people are beautiful. Not in looks.
Not in what they say. Just in what they are.

——MARKUS ZUSAK

It's so easy to get caught up in the superficial beauty of our world. It's incredible how you can meet someone so physically stunning and when you get to know them, they seem to lack basic kindness and compassion for others. The moment someone isn't kind to others, any physical beauty they might have had disappears. Real beauty comes from kindness, virtue, and compassion. Seeing that kind of beauty requires more than just a casual glance.

Goal: Take time to get to know people and then decide how beautiful they are; you will become more beautiful in the process.

April 3

Always remember, actions speak louder than words.

I continually strive to be better by evaluating my daily actions and how they affect other people. When I realize that my actions may have hurt someone, I make a point to go to them and apologize. It feels good when I make a conscious effort to recognize my faults and then do everything I can to make them right and demonstrate my love. These actions are so much more impactful than words.

Goal: Think about someone you should reach out to, whether it is to apologize or reconnect, tell them that you love them or that you are sorry.

Gold cannot be pure, and people cannot be perfect.

—CHINESE PROVERB

It's so important to acknowledge your weaknesses and imperfections. It may seem hard at first, but once you begin to recognize and come to peace with your weaknesses, you actually have an honest place to start improving. We shouldn't strive for perfection because it doesn't exist. When we accept others for who they are and love ourselves unconditionally (flaws and all), we have an opportunity to be open, to be courageous, and to learn.

Goal: Look at your weaknesses and think about how you can improve in a healthy way.

April 5

Slow and steady enjoys the race.

—MIKE BAYER

We always hear "Slow and steady wins the race," and though I love this idea, I actually love the idea of slowing down to savor the little moments in life even more. Living in our fast-paced world today, it's easy to get into a busy routine and sometimes we literally don't have time to catch our breath. Not only is this not healthy for our bodies and our stress levels, but it takes the joy out of whatever we're doing.

I've found that time goes quickly, and if I don't stop and slow down, I miss the little moments. So whatever place you're rushing to or goal you are rushing to get, remember to enjoy the process too—otherwise what's the point?

Goal: When you start to get wrapped up in your busy life, pause, take ten deep breaths, and try meditating or doing something that calms you down.

April 6

Nobody has ever measured, not even poets,
how much the heart can hold.

—ZELDA FITZGERALD

It truly is incredible how much love the heart can hold and there's no doubt in my mind that love is worth any pain and suffering that might come with it. For every heartache you have felt, think about all the amazing things that come with love, especially in the beginning: the butterflies in your stomach, the giddiness you feel all over your body. I wouldn't trade anything in the world for the way love makes me feel.

Goal: Open your heart and allow yourself to feel all emotions without the fear of getting hurt.

April 7

We are all just works in progress.

—MARY J. BLIGE, "WORK IN PROGRESS"

Nobody ever said you have to have it all figured it out because I promise you nobody does. What matters most is to keep working on yourself, keep allowing yourself to heal, grow, learn, and stay humble. Whenever you feel like your work is done, start all over again and remember that all of it is worth it.

Goal: Think about how you are a work in progress. Think about how much you have grown and changed in the last year. Imagine how you'll continue to change each year for the rest of your life. What is something about yourself that you can work on today?

Recovery is something that you have
to work on every single day, and it's
something that doesn't get a day off.

Being in recovery isn't always easy. I have good days and days
when I feel like giving up, but those are the days I know I have to
ask for help, which isn't easy. Whether it's a physical addiction, a
mental health issue, a disability, or an emotional trauma, we all
have things we're working through. The goal isn't to be perfect.
It's just to be the healthiest version of yourself—inside and out.

Goal: What traumas are you recovering from? What issues
are you working through? Reach out to a friend or seek professional help to support yourself.

April 9

I think it's very healthy to spend time alone.
You need to know how to be alone and not
be defined by another person.

—OLIVIA WILDE

It's not always easy to be alone. As I've come to spend more quality time alone it's not only become easier, but I have started really enjoying my solitude. Whether you are an introvert or an extrovert, it's really important to find peace and joy in alone time. When we really get to know ourselves alone, we become stronger people and better friends and overall better people.

Goal: Find comfort in spending time alone with your thoughts.

April 10

Loneliness and the feeling of being unwanted is the most terrible poverty.

—MOTHER TERESA

It doesn't matter how much money you have. Money doesn't provide anyone with love or kindness. Every single person wants to feel loved and cared for, and this has nothing to do with material wealth. All the money in the world doesn't matter, just the love and people that surround you.

Goal: Go out of your way to make someone feel wanted and loved today. Focus on being wealthy in love.

April 11

Set goals and dream big.

Having really big dreams is wonderful, but in order to achieve them you have to start setting goals and writing them down. It's not enough just to think about them, you have to actively pursue them. The best feeling is crossing one of your goals off your list after you've worked so hard to achieve a dream.

Goal: Make a list of your goals for the year. Stay focused and start making strides to cross them off your list.

April 12

Be the change you wish to see in the world.

—UNKNOWN

The more you act out what you wish to see in the world, the more you'll inspire others to do the same. It really is that simple. If you want to change, you have to *be* the change that's needed.

Goal: Make a list of things you believe in and don't be afraid to stand up for what you're passionate about.

I myself am made of flaws stitched together with good intentions.

—AUGUSTEN BURROUGHS

Each and every one of us has their cracks and their flaws. We never had the intention of going out and becoming flawed, but that's what happens in life—we make mistakes and we learn from them. That's what makes us who we are.

Goal: Be kinder and gentler with yourself. Accept your flaws, and be grateful for what you've learned from them.

April 14

How wonderful it is that nobody need wait a single moment before starting to improve the world.

—ANNE FRANK

I was walking by a homeless man recently and I watched as people walked past him. It made me so sad, so I stopped and talked to him. After I introduced myself, he told me his name was Denny. We started talking and laughing as he told me some jokes. After a while, he started to tear up and thank me. I asked him why and he told me it was the first time in days that anyone had spoken to him. He said he was so happy and thankful just to have the interaction with another person. I couldn't believe how such a simple thing brought both of us so much joy. I will never forget that moment.

Goal: Do one thing for someone else today to make their day brighter.

No need to worry about tomorrow, when we've been blessed with today.

I know that everybody worries about what's coming next, but in my experience it doesn't do any good. It just makes you more stressed out and usually you're just worrying about things that may never even happen. Today and this moment is all we have, so stay present and focused and count your blessings for today and trust that the rest will fall into place.

Goal: Count your blessings today.

April 16

Do something. Your future self will thank you for it.

——NIKE AD

All the decisions you make today in your life affect you in the long run. The things that you're telling yourself, the things you're putting in your body, the people you're surrounding yourself with—they stay with you. Whether it be ten days or ten years from now, it's important to be mindful of how you treat yourself. With this in mind it is so important to think about the bigger picture.

Goal: Every time you have a self-destructive thought, tell yourself the exact opposite. Watch how quickly your behavior can change when you're being mindful and staying positive.

April 17

How I feel about myself is more important than how I look. Feeling confident, being comfortable in your own skin—that's what really makes you beautiful.

—BOBBI BROWN

Nobody else has exactly what you have; you were given your body and your features, so be grateful you have them. My friend Spencer West has gone his entire life without legs, but that hasn't stopped him from truly living his life. Now, when I start to criticize my body, I think of Spencer's incredible strength and realize how lucky I am to have legs at all. If he can stand tall without legs, so can I.

Goal: Place yourself in someone else's shoes and appreciate what you have.

April 18

Be here now.

—RAM DASS

All we have is now. I've learned that after doing so many functions and performances and barely remembering them. It's because I wasn't living in the moment. I wasn't present in what I was doing.

Goal: Set aside all distractions, come out from behind your phone or computer, and enjoy the moment for exactly what is.

April 19

You're only as strong as your weakest member; you're only as positive as your most negative friend.

—KELLY ROWLAND

You are who your friends are, so make sure you know who you're hanging out with and what their values are. It's important to remember how our friends have such a powerful influence on us and vice versa. This can be a great thing as long as your friends surround you with love, loyalty, respect, and positivity.

Goal: Is there anyone in your life who has been making you feel bad about yourself? If there is, it might be a good time to have a heart-to-heart with that person and find out how to fix the situation.

April 20

When one door closes, another opens;
but we often look so long and so regretfully
upon the closed door that we do not see
the one that has opened for us.

—ALEXANDER GRAHAM BELL

No matter what you're going through, there's a light at the end of the tunnel. It may seem hard to get to it, but you can do it. Just keep working toward it and you'll find the positive side of things. I've realized that I can always find something to look forward to. Big or small, it helps to get me through those rough patches.

Goal: Remember that the bad will pass and soon you'll make it through to the other side.

April 21

May you live as long as you want
and not want as long as you live.

—TRADITIONAL IRISH SAYING

Our lives consist of the beauty we fill them with—the more beauty we surround ourselves with, the richer our lives will be. But wanting everything more and more blocks us from enjoying the things we already have. It's good to want things in life, but it's also important not to be greedy.

Goal: Don't obsess over what you don't have; feel grateful for all that you do have.

April 22

Remember how far you've come,
not just how far you have to go. You are
not where you want to be, but neither
are you where you used to be.

—RICK WARREN

Most of our lives move at such an accelerated pace we don't
always have the time to stop and reflect on how far we've come.
We are usually too busy looking ahead. But it's so important to
keep checking in with yourself. We change all the time. It's easy
to get caught up feeling dissatisfied with where you are when
you don't take the time to appreciate how far you've come. You
don't have to be exactly where you want to be, but the fact that
you are on your way is remarkable. Good things and progress
take time.

Goal: Make today all about celebrating how far you've come in
your life since last year. What is something you've changed in
your life that you are proud of?

April 23

Nobody is perfect. As long as we continue
to strive to be better, our imperfections
are part of our journey.

How many times have we done something "wrong" and then
regretted it later? As long as we learn something from it, the experience is not wasted. We aren't perfect; we are here to learn from
our mistakes and imperfections, not beat ourselves up for them.

Goal: Think about how to alter your regrets into lessons for
the future.

April 24

Underneath it's all the same love.

—MACKLEMORE, "SAME LOVE"

For all our individual eccentricities and unique gifts, we're still made up of the same flesh and blood. We are united and connected equally by our differences as well as our similarities. No matter how differently each of us goes about living our lives, we are all on a journey learning how to know and love ourselves as well as others with greater depth and honesty.

Goal: Focus on what connects you to your friends, family, and colleagues today.

April 25

Let yourself imagine exactly what you want your life to look like—fearlessly and with the courage to bring your dreams to fruition.

Our imaginations and the visions we allow ourselves to have are very significant. It's important for all of us to feel that we can make our dreams come true; I deeply believe that we can. But it takes work to do this; it doesn't just magically happen. So let your imagination run wild with everything you want your life to be rather than laughing it away because it seems unfathomable. Embrace your vision for your life, and allow it to be the daily goal you are moving toward. It's in your head for a reason.

Goal: Make a list of dreams you want to achieve someday.

April 26

It's so important to listen and be open to
the wisdom of our ancestors. We should
respect the teachings and words of
those who came before us.

Looking back at history, there are so many incredible, inspiring
stories from our own family trees and from our history books
that we just take for granted. But those people paved the way for
where we are today. It's important not only to learn from them
but to remember and show respect and gratitude for all that they
have done for us.

Goal: Open up a history book or find a historical figure online
that you know nothing about and learn something new. While
you're at it, ask someone in your family about one of your great-
grandparents—find out who they were and what they believed in.

April 27

Start where you are. Use what you have.
Do what you can.

—ARTHUR ASHE

Nobody is asking you to be perfect. It's enough to just do the best you can do today with what you have inside you right now. Oftentimes, we put too much pressure on ourselves to please other people.

Goal: Whatever you feel when you wake up is good enough; just start with that and make the most of today.

April 28

Most of us, I believe, admire strength . . .
Sometimes, though, I wonder if we confuse
strength with other words like aggression and
even violence.

—FRED ROGERS, *Mr. Rogers' Neighborhood*

Too often people confuse strength with violence. I think the kids who bullied me, and bullies in general, are hiding from their true pain by exerting a false sense of strength by belittling others. If more people would honor their feelings and admit to feeling weak, sad, or powerless, then they would have the opportunity to start healing. This kind of openness and honesty takes true strength and courage.

Goal: Be strong today for yourself or for someone else.

April 29

One of the greatest joys in life is watching a child laugh.

There's something about the innocence of a child laughing that never ceases to make my entire week. Children live in such a small world full of wonder. They haven't seen, for the most part, some of the sad things about the world going on around them that adults have. When our world opens up, we witness more and more. Good and bad. So just seeing a child laugh at the simplest things makes us nostalgic for that simpler time of life. It's great to fondly remember childhood, but don't stress yourself out thinking about what used to be. Enjoy where you are now as well.

Goal: If you have the opportunity, make a child laugh today.

April 30

Singing is a way of escaping. It's another world. I'm no longer on earth.

——EDITH PIAF

Since I was a young child, my voice always allowed me to escape and to find bliss wherever I was. Everyone has their own bliss in life and it often occurs when you lose yourself in the moment by completely immersing yourself into something. Just like Edith Piaf, I find that when I sing, I too soar and forget everything else.

Goal: Find what makes you happiest and allow yourself to soar beyond the clouds even with your feet planted right here on earth.

May

May 1

Be curious, not judgmental.

—WALT WHITMAN

It's so important to maintain the curiosity and sense of wonder that we have when we are young. When we are babies, we experience everything for the first time: crawling, eating, walking, talking, and sensations. As we get older we start to take simple things for granted. The more we're willing to stay open and remain curious about the world around us, the more we can discover and learn.

Goal: Be an explorer today. Don't take anything you see, hear, or touch for granted. Be willing to look more closely at everything and become a student of your environment.

May 2

Respect your mind, body, and soul.
You are WORTH it.

We are always the first ones to get down on ourselves. We are our own harshest critics. And a big part of our journey is learning how to love ourselves. That means taking good care of your mind, body, soul, and spirit. Treat yourself the way you would treat a little kid and see what a difference it makes. When you are kinder to yourself, everything will change for the better.

Goal: Stand in front of the mirror today and tell yourself you are a beautiful person.

May 3

Our lives begin to end the day we become silent about things that matter.

—MARTIN LUTHER KING JR.

It's important to give back, because if you never stand up for what you believe in, nobody else is going to. What if you're here on this earth to help make an important discovery, but you didn't value your thoughts enough to do anything?

Goal: Stand up for the things you believe in, live a life that is meaningful to you, and make sure you can sleep at night knowing you're doing your part to make this world a better place. There's no time like the present.

May 4

Let children read whatever they want and then talk about it with them. If parents and kids can talk together, we won't have as much censorship because we won't have as much fear.

—JUDY BLUME

It's so important that children feel like they can think and talk openly. Parents and teachers are meant to inspire young people—be role models to children and students. Don't put down their views and opinions. Let them know their value and intelligence.

Goal: No matter your age, make sure you always inspire, nurture, and support others.

May 5

Gay, straight, lesbian, bi: No one is
better than anyone else.

We are all equal. If anyone tries to tell you otherwise, you can
have an open conversation with them or walk away. Don't let
their prejudice and intolerance get the best of you.

Goal: Help spread tolerance in your community.

May 6

Don't ever settle.

People settle because they're afraid something better won't come along. They fear they aren't good enough. You are worth exactly what you want in life, but you have to believe it or you won't attract something better.

Goal: Take a moment to realize your worth.

May 7

Holding on to anger is like grasping a hot coal with the intent of throwing it at someone else; you are the one who gets burned.

—BUDDHA

I've had to learn this lesson many times in life because it's hard to let go. Anger and resentment are so toxic that you end up hurting yourself. When you are wronged, it's better to confront it with tolerance, forgiveness, and acceptance. Ultimately it's best to let it go, otherwise it builds up.

Goal: Write down all the things you are angry about on a piece of paper and burn it.

May 8

Sometimes, it is okay to be selfish.
Being selfless all the time can be
detrimental to your mind and body.

They say if you're in a plane and it's going down, you have to put
on your own oxygen mask before you put on anyone else's. You
can't take care of others if you aren't taking care of yourself first.
People think it's being selfish, but it's the good kind of selfish-
ness, the kind that enables you to give your truest, most authentic
self to be of service to others.

Goal: Do one loving thing for yourself today: Treat yourself
to a massage, sleep in, or meditate.

May 9

If you want to see the true measure
of a man, watch how he treats
his inferiors, not his equals.

—J. K. ROWLING

There's nothing more unattractive than when I see someone acting really nice to someone who has power and treating someone else badly because in their eyes they are lower on the social ladder. The best way to find out who someone really is, is to notice if they treat all people with equality. If they don't, it's worth reevaluating your relationship.

Goal: Treat all people the same, with love, respect, and kindness, regardless of their financial or social position in life. You are no better or worse than anyone else because of what you have or don't have.

May 10

Like the moon, come out from behind the clouds! Shine.

—BUDDHA

We all have bad days, but the darkness always brings light. You have the choice and the power to emerge from whatever darkness or hardship might be consuming you. Use your inner light to shine and light up the world. Sometimes it can be as simple as thinking happy thoughts or smiling when you don't want to.

Goal: Light up the world with your smile even if you're feeling down.

May 11

My mother said to me, "If you are a soldier, you will become a general. If you are a monk, you will become the pope." Instead I was a painter and became Picasso.

—PABLO PICASSO

I would not be where I am today if not for the love, friendship, and support of my amazing mother. She has always believed in me even when I didn't believe in myself. That sense of belief in me has given me so much courage to chase and live out my dreams.

My mom has taught me how to act with integrity, loyalty, strength, and love. I realize that I'm extremely fortunate and blessed to have such an amazing mom.

Goal: Tell someone in your life you're thankful for all the love they've provided.

May 12

When we are consumed by what other people think of us, we allow them to dictate how we live our lives, and then without realizing it, we lose touch with who we are.

We all want to be liked and loved, but when we focus on this instead of making sure we love ourselves first, we get lost in other people's opinions and we stop living honestly. If someone calls you a name, don't let it bother you—don't react. Feeding into their drama will only negatively affect your character.

Goal: What makes you special and unique? Think about one of your eccentricities and embrace it every day.

Don't torment yourself with jealousy.
It's a silly illusion that someone's life is
better than yours when the truth is that
each one of us is on a different path.

There are times in life when I let myself get completely consumed with jealousy for someone else's life, their body, their wardrobe, their talent. It's a common emotion to experience. They call it the green-eyed monster for a reason. It's self-destructive and when it's in the room, it consumes you. Be strong and don't focus on what other people have.

Goal: Release any jealousy you have for someone else's life and allow yourself to feel deep gratitude that you are living your own life.

May 14

Change is never painful, only the resistance to change is painful.

—BUDDHA

Change is a part of life and there's no way of getting around it. So accept that your life will be filled with all kinds of change, and even though it can sometimes feel uncomfortable, it's what builds our character and keeps us moving forward.

Goal: Embrace the changes going on in your life whether they're positive or negative. They're all moving you forward and starting a new chapter in your life comes with change. It's okay to be thankful for blessings.

May 15

You have the capability to change your life all with a simple shift in perspective.

Sometimes my day may start badly and I start to get down or frustrated. I even think, forget it—the day is ruined. It feels terrible and can cause me to be cranky and lash out, which affects others. I have learned that I can restart my day at any point. I simply sit quietly and reboot. I choose to shift my perspective and tell myself that the day that lies ahead of me is full of wonderful blessings and opportunities. I list ten or more things I appreciate in my life and that usually shifts my mood. Once my mood shifts, my entire day shifts like a chain reaction.

Goal: Start a daily gratitude notebook. List ten things you are most grateful for on a daily basis.

May 16

Don't forget to breathe.

It's an instinct we're born knowing, and yet for some reason it's the thing we forget the fastest, especially when we are stressed out and overwhelmed.

Goal: Focus on breathing in a peaceful place. It can really make a huge difference in brightening your day and your mood.

When someone whom I have helped,
Or in whom I have placed great hopes,
Mistreats me in extremely hurtful ways,
May I regard him still as my precious teacher.

—DALAI LAMA

Having compassion for others is so vital to our own happiness. We can always learn from people who have hurt us. It's not possible to go through life without getting hurt. Even our best friends who love us will make us feel angry from time to time. Your best friend is not a perfect friend, which is important to remember. People around you are human too. They make mistakes and that's important to remember.

Goal: Learn from everyone, even the people who hurt and disappoint you.

May 18

Go confidently in the direction of your dreams. Live the life you have imagined.

—UNKNOWN

If anyone tells you that you can't live the life you imagined, you don't have to prove them wrong—just keep on working your hardest and know in your heart that you can achieve it. Use their doubtful attitude as motivation.

Goal: You deserve all the happiness in the world, so pursue it with all the madness and passion in your soul.

We can't always rely on others to make us feel happy. We must first find it in ourselves.

I have come to realize that making yourself happy is most important. Never be ashamed of what you feel because we all feel the same emotions at one point or another. Maybe we express them in different ways, but fundamentally it's the same, which is why we can relate to each other. The main thing to remember is *never* let anyone make you feel bad about how you're feeling.

Goal: If you're having a bad day—don't count on others to cheer you up. Find happiness within yourself.

May 20

Whenever I climb, I am followed by a dog called ego.

—NIETZSCHE

As we come into our own in life and begin to climb up our personal ladders of success, we must be cautious to leave our egos behind and not allow them to interfere with the integrity and honesty of our work. Your ego will always be close behind, chasing you, nipping at your heels as you move up in this world. So don't let it get ahead of you.

Goal: Evaluate where your ego currently stands. Be aware of it and don't let it overpower you.

A smile can save a life.

Did you know that there's scientific evidence that smiling can boost your immune system and help you live a longer and happier life, not to mention that it makes the people around you happier too because smiling is contagious? There was a time I was going through security at an airport and out of nowhere a TSA agent smiled at me, and it changed my entire day. When you make someone else's day brighter, it makes your day better too.

Goal: Smile often—you never know whose day you will brighten. You never know the impact one smile will have on someone's life.

May 22

When you throw dirt, you lose ground.

—TEXAN PROVERB

Life is all about choices. We always have a choice in how we respond to offensive people. The most tempting thing in the world is to respond with the same kind of behavior we are offended by. Ask yourself what it would really achieve.

Goal: The next time someone insults you, calmly inquire how they would feel if you said the same thing to them.

May 23

True joy comes when you inspire,
encourage, and guide someone else
on a path that benefits him or her.

—ZIG ZIGLAR

There are a lot of jealous people out there. Sometimes your happy news creates tension in a relationship. Be sure to be supportive and happy with their news and, hopefully, it will be reciprocated.

Goal: The next time a friend or family member shares good news with you, make sure your joy is sincere.

May 24

Change happens by listening and then starting a dialogue with the people who are doing something you don't believe is right.

—JANE GOODALL

There are over 7 billion people in this world, yet each of us has only one brain and one set of values and opinions. No matter how educated, compassionate, kind, open, and willing we are, there are still going to be plenty of times when we are wrong. We can't get self-righteous about our values and shut out other opinions or belief systems even if we don't agree with them.

Goal: Stay open-minded, be comfortable with being wrong. Broaden your horizons with new areas of interest. It's more beneficial to you to open your mind and consider a different perspective.

I walk slowly, but I never walk backward.

—ABRAHAM LINCOLN

Recovery is a process—no matter what it is you're overcoming. No one is better or greater for recovering faster. It's not a race. You need to go at your own pace, even if that is pace is slow. There will be days when you feel like giving up—don't. There will be days when you're at risk of relapsing—don't. So long as you set your own pace and never go backward in your recovery, you're making tremendous progress, and that's all that matters. So be proud of what you've accomplished for yourself.

Goal: Don't compare your recovery process to others. Remember that each of us heals physically, mentally, and emotionally at the pace that's right for ourselves. Give yourself the time you need and deserve.

May 26

Time goes by so fast, people go in and out of your life. You must never miss the opportunity to tell these people how much they mean to you.

—UNKNOWN

Loss is a part of life. Over the years I've lost several people who are dear to my heart. Nothing can ever bring them back but when I think of them, their values and virtues, I can keep their spirit alive within me and that is a meaningful feeling. The most important thing to remember, however, is to make the most of the precious time we have with the ones we love.

Goal: Light a candle or say a prayer for someone you love today who is no longer with you.

May 27

At this moment I am exactly
where I need to be.

I used to resist everything and I didn't trust my higher power. With my recovery and my willingness to change, I now see that I am exactly where I'm supposed to be. In this present moment is where I find my happiness.

Goal: Think about where you are in your life today: accomplishments, relationships, career, and be happy for the life you've built.

May 28

Parents can only give good advice or put them on the right paths, but the final forming of a person's character lies in their own hands.

—ANNE FRANK

So much of my journey thus far has been informed by my parents, their gifts and their flaws. I realized after my recovery that I can learn from my parents, and it's up to me to make my life what I want it to be.

Goal: Thank your parents for giving you the gift of life and doing their best.

Humility is not thinking less of yourself,
it's thinking of yourself less.

——C. S. LEWIS

A lot of people are skeptical about giving a homeless person money. One thing you can do is buy a homeless person a meal or a bottle of water so at least you know they will get something nutritious to eat or drink. I once saw a homeless man and remembered that I had a snack in my purse. I went up to him and said, "I don't want to offend you, but if you're hungry, I'd love to give this to you." He reacted like he had won the lottery. I couldn't believe how something so simple could make him so happy.

Goal: Go out of your way to help a homeless person, or someone else in need, today.

May 30

You can't use up creativity. The more you use the more you have.

——MAYA ANGELOU

I remember after I wrote my first few songs I was worried that more might never come out. I didn't realize at the time the only way to experience more creativity was to just keep creating.

Goal: Don't be cautious with your creativity—let it out. Some of it will be extraordinary and some mediocre. Never stop trying.

May 31

You are destined to be God's child.

—ANONYMOUS

Each and every one of us is on this earth for a reason. No two people are alike. We are all perfectly made and created to do what we're meant to do in this world. You are precious, you are unique, and you are special, so don't let anyone tell you otherwise.

Goal: Celebrate the ways in which you are special and unique.

June

June 1

The most courageous act is still
to think for yourself. Aloud.

—COCO CHANEL

Each one of us is born with a unique and remarkable gift that's not only meant to change our lives but the greater world around us. I know this to be true because I've witnessed it throughout my life. Whatever your strengths are, they may be something that someone else wishes they had. So use your gifts wisely and you will be amazed how much you can inspire others.

Goal: Inspire someone today just by being yourself.

June 2

No one is perfect, but we can all strive to be better people.

Life is a journey and a process that is constantly presenting us with new opportunities to grow and evolve. Every day and every year offers a chance to continue to be stronger, happier, and more compassionate.

Goal: Set an intention to better yourself and be an inspiration to those around you.

June 3

Forever—is composed of Nows—

—EMILY DICKINSON

Stop searching for the next great thing. You are in it right now. The next moment will come to you when it's ready as long as you stay present. It's human nature to constantly be distracted by everything we want in life, where we're going next, and what we've left behind. Focus on where you're at right now with all you have.

Goal: Absorb the moment you're in and commit it to memory.

June 4

You have everything you need inside you. The key is living honestly so you can connect and be in touch with who you really are.

A huge part of my recovery was learning that I didn't need to search outside of myself. I had the answers and the inner peace within me. When we finally realize this—it becomes so liberating.

Goal: Stand in front of the mirror today and tell yourself, "I have everything I need inside me."

June 5

Our deepest fear is not that we are inadequate.
Our deepest fear is that we are powerful
beyond measure. It is our light, not our
darkness, that most frightens us.

—MARIANNE WILLIAMSON

It can feel very scary sometimes when you realize what you are
capable of in this world. Each of us is born with our own inherent
power to accomplish extraordinary things in life. They say with
great power comes great responsibility, so own your responsibility to do something wonderful with your life—cherish it.

Goal: Use what you have, your resources, to do something
meaningful today.

June 6

Don't cry because it's over; smile because it happened.

—DR. SEUSS

There will be times when something good comes to an end. Instead of thinking about the fact that it's over—stay positive that it happened in the first place. I was so sad to return home after spending time in Africa with my friends and family. We were all crying when it was time to go—no one wanted to leave such an amazing place. I can look back now, though, without crying. I'm so thankful for my time spent there with people I love, and I can't wait to go back.

Goal: Think about a happy moment in your life and be grateful for the joy it gave you. Reflect on happy moments, even if they've passed.

June 7

I am half agony, half hope.

—JANE AUSTEN

A sound support system is important for everyone to have. There have been times when I'm dealing with some heavy things, but what helped me see happiness again was the faith my fans had in me and the hope they gave me. I learned that I have so much support from my fans and the people around me. I can't explain how happy that makes me.

Goal: Give hope to someone struggling. Tell them you're there for them.

June 8

Love isn't a state of perfect caring. It is an active noun, like struggle. To love someone is to strive to accept that person exactly the way he or she is, right here and now.

——FRED ROGERS, *Mister Rogers' Neighborhood*

One of the hardest things about relationships is accepting the other person for who they are. I can't tell you how many times I've wanted to change one thing or another about a friend or a loved one, but then I remember that nobody is perfect, including me.

Goal: If you find yourself criticizing someone, be mindful that no one is perfect—yourself included.

June 9

A world so hateful some would rather
die than be who they are.

—MACKLEMORE, "SAME LOVE"

There are so many young people who are taking their own lives because bullies are making them feel worthless. As someone who was bullied, I know how destructive and devastating it can be when kids say horrible things. With cyberbullying, people feel even freer to hide behind their computers and say the most hateful things. It's up to each and every one of us to take a stand for anyone being bullied or ripped apart by cruel words.

Goal: Stand up for someone today and make sure they know how valuable they are to this world.

June 10

Don't wait around for other people to be happy for you. Any happiness you get, you've got to make yourself.

—ALICE WALKER

You can't fully love anybody until you love yourself. As great as it feels being in a relationship, at the end of the day, if you're not happy with yourself, having a boyfriend or girlfriend won't change that. You're only going to be with your significant other while you're awake. It's your consciousness that falls asleep on your pillow every night, not theirs.

Goal: Whether you are single or in a relationship, spend some quality time bonding with and getting to know yourself even better.

You don't deserve a point of view if the only thing you see is you.

—PARAMORE, "PLAYING GOD"

There are many people who walk around with big egos feeling righteous and more entitled than others. It doesn't matter where you come from or who you think you are, we're all human beings with beating hearts. A lot of times people judge others and assume that they're right, but you can't just assume your point of view is right. You have to be willing to see outside of yourself. There are so many people in the world and if you're only asking yourself for answers, then you're living your life in a bubble.

Goal: Think twice before you feel like judging someone, put yourself in their shoes and remember they're entitled to their own opinions and perspectives. They see the world differently.

June 12

It is not in the stars to hold our
destiny but in ourselves.

—WILLIAM SHAKESPEARE

We always have choices in life. We make our opportunities, and we must find it in ourselves to achieve our destiny. We never really know what we can do or achieve unless we try.

Goal: Stop leaving something important up to chance. Take control of it, and create the outcome you want.

June 13

Without self-love and self-acceptance I would be nowhere.

Learning to love and accept yourself for who you are is not an easy thing to do. I learned so much about myself in treatment and during my recovery. It allowed me to discover the power of self-love and self-acceptance. I'm still learning every day. But at the end of the day I must love myself before anyone else can love me. Learning how to do this was hard, but it has made all the difference.

Goal: Find the part of you that you dislike the most and start loving it.

June 14

I am large, I contain multitudes.

——WALT WHITMAN

One of the reasons I was so unhappy for years was because I never embraced my emotions; I was always trying to stay in control. I couldn't see it at first, but I was making it even worse by not giving my emotions the attention they needed. What I thought was keeping me sane was actually making me lose myself and feel totally out of control, but once I started to embrace my feelings, I started to feel whole again.

Goal: What emotion have you been running from? Stop, take a deep breath, and allow yourself to feel it. It might feel worse at first, but once you let it in, it's not so scary.

June 15

You will find it necessary to let things go simply for the reason that they are heavy.

—C. JOYBELL C.

Every day brings new opportunities to grow, and part of that growth means accepting that there are certain things we cannot change. When we hold on to or obsess about the things we cannot change, we lose ourselves.

When we let go, we free our hearts, minds, and bodies for something even greater. When I cleared that space in my heart, so many wonderful things started coming my way.

Goal: Let something or someone toxic that you've been holding on to go. If you need to, throw something out that you've been holding on to, or write a letter to someone you are trying to let go of.

We often look outside ourselves for answers, for happiness, for a chance to feel whole.

When I was consumed by my addictions, I realize now, I was looking outside of myself for answers, happiness, peace, and love. I didn't know at the time that this was causing me so much pain. My recovery taught me that I have to find the answers and strength within myself.

Goal: Think about what it is you really want and not what others expect of you.

Only do what your heart tells you to.

—PRINCESS DIANA

There are plenty of moments in our lives when we struggle with making decisions, whether they're small or large. Our heart can be telling us one thing, our head another, and our friends something entirely different. It's important to weigh all options, then do what your heart truly believes is right. Don't just do what your friends are telling you to do—you must make your own decisions based on your intuition.

Goal: Next time you have to make a decision, weigh all the options—especially those of the heart.

Do just once what others say
you can't do, and you will never pay
attention to their limitations again.

——CAPT. JAMES R. COOK

One of the most liberating feelings in the world is showing some-one who didn't believe in you what you are capable of. The first time you experience this amazing feeling you'll learn that it's a waste of time listening to people who tell you what you can't do. Better to spend your time showing them and yourself what you CAN do. Remember, the sky's the limit.

Goal: Do one thing someone has always told you that you couldn't.

June 19

With pain, suffering, and grief come many opportunities to grow and change as long as we stay open.

When your faith and strength are challenged, you have the most incredible opportunity to grow. It's up to you what you make of it. Sometimes it's hard to ask for help, but it never hurts to receive it. I've made a vow to myself that when times are difficult I will reach out for help and embrace that part of my journey with an open mind. I know that these obstacles are a way to become stronger and develop my faith, but I can't do it without staying open to receiving help from others.

Goal: If you're dealing with something painful, stay open-minded and ask for help. You never need to face anything alone—there are so many resources available to help.

June 20

Happiness does not depend on what
you have or who you are; it solely
relies on what you think.

—BUDDHA

Each one of us has the capacity to experience deep joy, but it
sometimes takes work. If you've been feeling down, take a look
at the kinds of thoughts you've been having. Maybe even write
them down just so you can really see the way you currently view
life. If you find that your thoughts are more negative than positive, you have to make a conscious effort to start changing them.

Goal: Make a list of all your negative thoughts and then write
out the opposite thought for each one. Stand in front of the mirror and read the positive thoughts out loud to yourself.

June 21

You are here for a reason. Use your gifts.

Whatever gifts you've been blessed with, use them to make the world a better place. Nobody else has what you have so apply your thoughts and ideas to help change the world. You never know how you can impact this world unless you believe in yourself and try to make a difference.

Goal: Take the causes you feel strongest about and do something to help or benefit them.

The pain passes, but the beauty remains.

—PIERRE-AUGUSTE RENOIR

When we're going through trying and difficult times, it's hard to imagine anything but the immense suffering we are in. But there is always a light at the end of the tunnel. I have learned the pain always passes, but the beauty that comes from your transformation will last forever. Know that one day you'll be able to look back and appreciate what you've grown from.

Goal: Don't immerse yourself in the pain—it will pass.

June 23

Too many of us are not living our dreams because we are living our fears.

—LES BROWN

Fears stop you from all things possible. Don't let fear get in the way of anything, especially your dreams. Did you know that FEAR is actually an acronym that stands for False Evidence Appearing Real? In other words, your fears are not real because they're not actually happening—they're based on things that haven't happened yet and therefore don't exist.

Goal: Replace a fear with a wish or a dream for your life and choose to focus on that instead.

What we think, we become.

—BUDDHA

Our thoughts are so powerful that we must always be mindful and conscious of what we're telling ourselves. We have the power to manifest anything we want with the power of our thinking. So often we can get into a pattern of negative thinking without even realizing it, and before we know it we have brought into our lives the very thing we were afraid of. The good news is that this principle also works for positive thoughts. By thinking wonderful things about our lives we are subconsciously changing them with the energy of our perspective.

Goal: Make sure you spend today thinking thoughts aligned with your dreams. Cut out the thoughts that are bringing you down.

June 25

I choose not to be a victim.

It would be pretty easy for me to play the victim with everything in my life that I've been through, but that doesn't help me nor would it inspire anyone else. It's my choice to let my past experiences teach and empower me so that I can help others.

Goal: Think about something traumatic that happened in your life and find a way to use it for the greater good.

June 26

Be nice to nerds; chances are you'll
end up working for one.

—BILL GATES

Always treat others with the kindness you wish to receive. Someone's social status, or any standing, should never influence how you treat them. But that should never be a reason to treat anyone differently. You should always treat others with kindness and love.

Goal: Never assume someone is less than you, or you become less than them.

June 27

If you don't know where you are going, any road will get you there.

—LEWIS CARROLL

It's more important to have the will to grow and stay open to all the infinite possibilities than to know exactly where you're going. That will change as you change.

Goal: Stay open to any and all possibilities that present themselves to you. You never know where success and joy will turn up.

June 28

If you don't love yourself for your
flaws and imperfections, you can't
expect anyone else to either.

Sometimes the very thing we are most insecure about is the
feature that people like the most about us. You're not supposed
to look like everyone else. We are each made differently, so
find whatever flaw or imperfection you have and start embracing it because it's part of you.

Goal: Be proud of your originality. There's no one else in
the world that's like you.

June 29

Only surround yourself with people who you can communicate with.

Communication is vital to every relationship. There are people out there whose personalities just don't mix with yours. Don't waste your time trying to figure out why. Just go where you are wanted and understood, and everything else will fall into place.

Goal: If there's someone in your life you are having trouble communicating with, try to work it out. Be sure the tone in your voice comes from a place of love and respect to connect with them.

June 30

We must let go of the life we have planned, so as to accept the one that is waiting for us.

—JOSEPH CAMPBELL

It's good to have ideas, plans, and dreams, but they won't always turn out as you imagine. Building up elaborate scenarios in your head can end in disappointment, so it's always best to keep an open mind and anticipate change.

Goal: It can be trying, but accept what life hands you.

July

July 1

Life is short, so you have to do what you love. There's no time to waste.

I vividly remember being five years old and wanting to be a superstar—to be the next Shirley Temple. I fell in love with singing, dancing, and acting and I was determined to make it. I'm thankful that I started dreaming big at such a young age because it allowed me to focus on exactly what I wanted. However old you are, you have to chase that dream down until it's yours. Dreams don't come when you're just sitting around waiting for them to happen. It's never perfect and it may never be just how you imagined. But you have to do what makes you happy.

Goal: Stop putting off an important dream. Do what you can to achieve it.

July 2

When we see men of a contrary character, we should turn inward and examine ourselves.

—CONFUCIUS

Often when the actions or behaviors of others bother us, it's a reflection of something we are wrestling with about ourselves. We tend to see a mirror image of our struggles in someone else. If we acknowledge and address this, especially to ourselves, we won't project our battles onto others. It's interesting when we dig deep and ask ourselves what's bothering us. Sometimes, what we find is quite interesting.

Goal: What quality or characteristic of a friend or family member has been driving you crazy? Think about how it might be more related to you than you realized and just start working on it.

July 3

Every child is an artist. The problem is how
to remain an artist once he grows up.

——PABLO PICASSO

Keeping your sense of innocence, youth, and freedom is vital to
staying happy. We're all artists who have been given the inherent
power to create and shape our own lives. With this in mind it's
vital to never lose your sense of carefree wonder and curiosity
about yourself and the world around you.

Goal: Growing up doesn't mean you have to forfeit hobbies to
become mature. Always leave time for the things you've always
enjoyed.

July 4

For to be free is not merely to cast off one's chains, but to live in a way that respects and enhances the freedom of others.

—NELSON MANDELA

Part of living truthfully and honestly is ensuring that others around you are also able to live with the same physical and emotional freedoms. Fortunately we live in a free country, but there are social injustices that take place every day, not only in America but all over the world. It's part of our responsibility as compassionate human beings to do all we can to ensure and enhance the freedom of those around us.

Goal: Don't take your freedom for granted; embrace yours and help others around you to do the same.

July 5

The best medicine for embarrassment is the confidence to laugh at yourself.

There have been so many times when I've fallen onstage. The truth is that I'm just a clumsy person and it's something I've learned to embrace and even love. Every time I fall onstage, I can choose to be embarrassed and run away or I can land, pose, and smile. If I can make people laugh before they laugh at me, then the fall doesn't hurt.

Goal: Laugh at yourself. Don't take everything so seriously.

July 6

Prayer is not an old woman's idle amusement. Properly understood and applied, it is the most potent instrument of action.

——MAHATMA GANDHI

A lot of people think that when you pray it needs to be a formal ritual in a church, synagogue, or mosque. When I pray, I talk to God like he's my best friend. I don't hold back what I'm feeling and I don't wait to be in a holy location. I know that wherever I am, it's good enough to be heard. Even if you don't believe in God and you're praying to the universe, you're being honest with yourself. Putting your energy into the world shows that you are open to change, to learn, and to receive help.

Goal: Say a prayer to whatever you believe in and ask for help or wisdom about something that's been weighing on you.

July 7

When we count our blessings instead of our problems everything changes for the better.

After treatment, I realized that I had to change my way of thinking about so many things. One of the biggest changes was to focus on all that I had instead of all that I didn't have. The more I focused on my blessings and the things and people I was grateful for, the more those blessings and people began to show up in my daily life. When you begin to visualize and hold powerful positive imagery in your mind, it appears almost like magic. This is the power of gratitude.

Goal: Make a list of the top five people in your life you can go to for anything.

July 8

No one deserves anything less than being loved.

We deserve to experience all forms of love. The people who act the most hateful and unworthy of being loved are the ones who were deprived of it growing up. It's up to each and every one of us to make sure we are giving those around us as much love as we are giving ourselves. The people who seem hateful and toxic are not necessarily people you should spend time with, but at the very least send them your positive thoughts.

Goal: Be grateful that you are able to feel, experience, give, and receive love. It is such a blessing.

July 9

Peace and love are eternal.

—JOHN LENNON

Sometimes I wish I could have lived in the sixties because it was such an incredible time in the world for music, civil rights, fashion, politics, and culture. But one of the most inspiring parts of that time period was the peace movement. To see so many people across generations band together in support of peace and love is so inspiring and beautiful to me. I hope and pray that we can continue to practice tolerance, kindness, compassion, peace, and love every day of our lives. We need it now more than ever and it is up to each and every one of us to practice and spread these values.

Goal: Spread the message of peace and love wherever you go. Give free hugs today.

July 10

Follow your bliss and the universe will open doors where there were only walls.

—JOSEPH CAMPBELL

In a world that is full of challenges and unknowns, the simplest rule of thumb for me is to do what makes me happy. The world opens up in unforeseen ways when you dare to think of all the possibilities. Do what makes you happy and good things will follow.

Goal: Pursue the things that give you the most fulfillment and happiness.

July 11

It is some relief to weep; grief is satisfied and carried off by tears

—OVID

No matter how strong or tough you think you are, each and every one of us needs to release our emotions. Some people cry a lot and others cry infrequently. But I know that when I really need to cry and then I finally do, I feel like a new person. It's a way for me to let go and release—to express my sadness.

Goal: It's not healthy to bottle up strong emotions, so allow yourself to release them.

July 12

The only thing that comes to a sleeping man is dreams.

—TUPAC

You have to work hard for what you want or your dreams will never actually happen. You can't just sit back and wait for something to happen. God helps those who help themselves and those who help themselves will succeed.

Goal: Each and every one of us has a purpose—make sure you are living out your dreams.

July 13

So go ahead. Fall down. The world
looks different from the ground.

——OPRAH WINFREY

Failures, mistakes, learning, and new beginnings are all a part of
life. If I had taken my need to go to rehab as a sign of failure, I
wouldn't be where I am today. Instead I made the choice to start
over, deal with my problems, and get back up again. Believe me,
it wasn't easy. There were times when it would have been easier
to give up and stay where I was. But sometimes we need to hit
rock bottom to see the way out. Our failures don't define us—
they shape us and we are all the better for that.

Goal: Think about what failures have shaped you for the
better.

July 14

Gratitude is the key to happiness.

I am so grateful to all of my friends, family, and fans who have helped me stay strong on my road to recovery. I feel such deep gratitude to every single person who has been strong for me because it has given me the strength I needed to come out of this and make my way toward recovery.

Goal: Today make a point to thank everyone around you for being in your life, especially the ones who've stuck by your side through tough times.

You should never apologize for your existence.

Too many times people will say sorry for things that they really don't need to apologize for. We all do it. When we startle someone, or when someone bumps into you, we say sorry when it wasn't our fault. We are just trying to be polite. But what you are actually doing is telling yourself that you're not worthy of standing right where you are! You deserve your place on earth, wherever that may be.

Goal: Be proud of where you are today and how far you've come on your journey. You are exactly where you are supposed to be.

July 16

Sometimes you have to lie. But to yourself you must always tell the truth.

—LOUISE FITZHUGH

Don't feel bad when you make a mistake because it's in the past and you definitely can't go back in time to fix it. But if you aren't honest with yourself about your mistake then you've done something wrong. We are all just going through this life together, learning as we go, but it's so important to admit when you've done something wrong, even if it was an accident. Just apologize, own it, move on, and free yourself.

Goal: Apologize to someone for a recent mistake you have made, no matter how big or small.

July 17

Always act like you're wearing an invisible crown.

—UNKNOWN

When we give so much of ourselves to our work it's really important to do our best. No matter what other people think of your creation, it's so important to celebrate your labors and creativity. Part of creativity is that we usually get better with more practice and experience. Each project you do will usually be better than the previous one. It's not about perfecting anything—it's about getting better.

Goal: No matter how you feel, don't forget to recognize your hard work, perseverance, and creativity.

July 18

Don't give in to your fears; if you do, you
won't be able to talk to your heart.

—PAULO COELHO

Love illuminates all things and fear distorts the truth and fills
your mind with negativity. Fear gives you an excuse to hide
behind your heart. Everyone has fear. It takes a lot more strength
to rise above your fear and lead with your heart.

Goal: Listen to your heart and trust your instincts.

July 19

You get in life what you have
the courage to ask for.

—OPRAH WINFREY

People will come in and out of your life. Not everyone's going to know how to make you feel good, but don't get hung up on that—just let it go. The people who stay are the ones who make you feel wonderful. But don't rely on others to make you happy, because sometimes you will be disappointed.

Goal: If someone has let you down, ask yourself—Will this matter a year from now? It'll help you let go and gain perspective.

July 20

Every man has his secret sorrows which
the world knows not; and oftentimes,
we call a man cold when he is only sad.

——HENRY WADSWORTH LONGFELLOW

Don't take anything personally. Whatever people say and do
isn't because of you, it's a projection of the way they are feeling
inside. When people are kind to you it is because they are kind
and loving to themselves. When people lash out at you with their
words and actions, it's not because you have done something bad
but because they are suffering themselves. Have mercy for those
who lash out at others. We don't know what they're struggling
with at home.

Goal: The next time someone says something that hurts you,
visualize it as a bead of water that rolls right off you.

July 21

All kids need is a little help, a little hope
and somebody who believes in them.

——MAGIC JOHNSON

Hope is such a powerful gift to give young people. So many children come from broken homes and they are deprived of love, emotional nourishment, and support. When you give a child hope they see all the dreams they're capable of.

Goal: Step out of yourself and sign up to volunteer with children who are less fortunate than you.

July 22

Not everything that is faced can be changed,
but nothing can be changed until it is faced.

—JAMES BALDWIN

The damage and the impact that bullying has made on my life is tremendous. There was a long period of time when I let the pain define who I was. It was important for me to find a balance between coming to terms with it all and letting go. I took a huge step when I confronted the girl who bullied me. I told her how her words scarred me and made me feel worthless. They ultimately led to other emotional and physical issues I'm still overcoming. She hardly remembered her actions and was convinced that I would have forgotten all about it now that I was successful. I was so shocked at our different perceptions, but more than anything I felt like a massive weight was lifted off my chest. I forgave her, which made me feel stronger and clearer, and that's exactly what I needed all along.

Goal: Think of someone from your past who has hurt you. Have compassion and look beyond their faults.

July 23

It is easier to prevent bad habits than to break them.

—BENJAMIN FRANKLIN

Now is the time to give up bad habits. They're only hindering your recovery. Sometimes we don't even realize what our bad habits do to us. We have a fear of letting them go, but now is the time to set them aside.

Goal: Do an inventory of your habits. Are they postively affecting your life?

July 24

Everything will be okay in the end,
if it's not okay, it's not the end.

—ANONYMOUS

When you find yourself going through difficult times, you may think life is over and ruined. But you're not even close. When I went into treatment I was convinced my life was over. I thought I wasn't going to have a career and that people wouldn't like me anymore. I thought it was the end, but really it was the first day of the rest of my life. No matter what you're going through, you can start over and find the positivity in a new beginning.

Goal: Give yourself time to process whatever you are going through in life. It's never too late to have a fresh beginning.

July 25

Your passion is infinite.

When you connect to the passion within you, there are no limitations. Passion is the driving force to any art and it's up to you to make something beautiful with your life.

Goal: Remind yourself that you are capable of great things with hard work.

July 26

Do your part to make this world
a better place.

I'm a firm believer in leaving this world a better place for future generations. Being a public figure has presented me with so many extraordinary opportunities to give back, to volunteer, and to touch so many lives along the way. I've had the privilege of advocating for children and adults all over the world dealing with bullying, eating disorders, and mental health issues. Everyone has causes close to their hearts, so whatever you're passionate about do something to make a difference.

Goal: Pick up the phone and volunteer at a local nonprofit organization.

July 27

Success is becoming who you really are.

—ANONYMOUS

One of the most challenging things in life is figuring out who you're meant to be. If you're already on a journey to become who you are—you're already a success because that's farther than most people.

Goal: Help a friend who feels lost. Maybe you can help them get on track to find their own identity.

July 28

Nobody is as powerful as we make them out to be.

—ALICE WALKER

Most of us, at one time or another, hide behind our favorite fictional character or mythology; for me it's always been Cinderella. She lives under the shadow of her sisters and is forced into servitude until one day her unfortunate circumstances are turned into fortune. When I was younger I was always known as Dallas Lovato's little sister. She never meant for me to feel this way, but I always felt like I was in her shadow. Even though I was so proud to call her my sister, I never felt like I could fully shine. It's taken a lot of work for me to feel like I can shine on my own. I realize that overcoming that obstacle was part of my journey in truly loving myself. Today I have a closer relationship with my sister, all because I let go of my envy towards her.

Goal: Don't be content in the shadow of anyone. Break out and love yourself.

July 29

Always have hope. The best feeling
in the world is knowing that there
are infinite possibilities.

—ANONYMOUS

In our darkest hours there's always a ray of light to be seen and a kernel of hope to be found. Grab onto that hope and let the excitement of all the possibilities motivate you.

Goal: When you're down, search for the glimmer of hope inside you and let your mind run wild with the promise of what's to come.

July 30

This too shall pass.

—ANONYMOUS

Reflecting on some of the painful experiences I've been through, I realize how hard it can be to overcome sadness and pain. I realize that time doesn't heal all wounds completely, but it helps the pain subside. No matter how long it takes, you will feel better at some point. You will accept what has passed.

Goal: However you're feeling today, know that things will get better, and let that make you happy for now. It *will* get better.

July 31

Be yourself, everyone else is already taken.

—OSCAR WILDE

We all have moments when we feel lost. We look to our friends, our colleagues, our roommates, and even to strangers thinking that maybe the answer to happiness is about being someone else or changing who we are. I promise you this will make you miserable. It's one thing to be inspired and influenced by someone who has good taste and good values. It's quite another to think that by becoming someone else you will be happier.

Goal: Be yourself today and every day.

August

August 1

Hope can get you through anything.

There have been so many times in my life when I've felt lost, broken, confused, and filled with pain. All of my ups and downs have taught me that I must always have faith. I know now that as long as I maintain my hope and my faith I will always be okay.

Goal: Think about a time in your life when you felt hopeless and remember how you got through it. Apply it to future struggles. You can get through anything.

August 2

Love is the answer, and you know that for sure.

—JOHN LENNON, "MIND GAMES"

All kinds of relationships require love and respect. Those things take time. Make sure you nurture the relationship that you have with yourself and the relationship you have with your family and friends. It's not enough just to say you love them. You have to put in time and effort and demonstrate your love through your words and your actions.

Goal: Show someone you love them with your actions. Sometimes saying "I love you" is not enough.

August 3

It takes courage to grow up and
become who you really are.

—E. E. CUMMINGS

Growing up is difficult, and just when we think we are done growing, we realize we've only just begun. When I went into treatment, I thought my problems were over and done. The truth is you must always keep working on yourself and your recovery. It's dangerously easy for us to get too comfortable, so it takes courage to move forward and accept change.

Goal: Rise above any obstacles placed in your way so that you may become the person that you really are.

August 4

For every action, there is an
equal and opposite reaction.

—NEWTON'S THIRD LAW OF MOTION

When my father passed away, I was filled with such a deep sense of loss and utter heartbreak. For all my pain, I knew there existed an equal sense of hope. It was important for me to honor my feelings, but also to use the pain I was in to do something magnificent.

My father and I didn't have the best relationship because he struggled with mental health issues and addiction, but I decided to honor him by starting the Lovato Scholarship at Cast Recovery to help one person at a time who is dealing with an addiction or mental health issue. This was my way of taking a tragic moment in my life and turning it into something positive.

Goal: The next time you are in a sad situation, find a way to turn it around to find the positive spin.

August 5

We are what we repeatedly do; excellence
then is not an act but a habit.

——ARISTOTLE

Anything you want to be wonderful at requires patience and practice. It's as simple as brushing our teeth, which we hardly think about because we do it three times a day. By repeatedly doing a healthy habit we make it a regular part of our routine. It's good to have healthy habits; the more you have, the better you will become. When you strive every day to be better, eventually you will be.

Goal: Figure out what you love and what is good for you and make it a habit.

August 6

We've got to live, no matter
how many skies have fallen.

——D. H. LAWRENCE

Things come to you for the right reasons at the right time so don't resist them. Surrender to these gifts and challenges with grace and ease.

Goal: Whatever you're fighting today, surrender to it.

August 7

I don't like to gamble, but if there's one thing
I'm willing to bet on, it's myself.

——BEYONCÉ

Recovery was a painful, humbling journey that allowed me to really know myself in a way I never thought possible. There's freedom in knowing and accepting that I will never be perfect. Recovery is a daily effort, and it's important that I continue to work hard at it. I can't get lazy about it or take things for granted but that's been part of the learning experience.

Goal: Whether you are in recovery or not, think about your journey and how you can continue to improve and enrich your life each and every day.

August 8

The voyage of discovery is not in seeking new
landscapes but in having new eyes.

——MARCEL PROUST

It's important to see the world with your eyes open. Always be
looking to find something new even in the most ordinary of
places. It's great to see the world, but it's all for nothing if you
aren't ready to see new things.

Goal: Try to see something or someone from a new perspective. Release all preconceived notions.

August 9

Remember only God can judge ya
Forget the haters cause someone loves ya

—MILEY CYRUS, "WE CAN'T STOP"

You can't please everyone. The only thing you can really focus on is living your life. If someone doesn't like what you do, just remember it's not personal and keep expressing yourself the way you want to.

Goal: Don't think about how people will perceive you or how you express yourself. As long as you're bettering yourself and making yourself happy, nothing else matters.

You have to learn how to communicate if you want to get along in this world.

When you learn how to communicate with others there's no problem you can't solve. It doesn't mean you'll always agree with other people and it certainly doesn't mean that they will agree with you. But none of that matters if you possess the maturity and the patience to work through your differences. Think about how much more peace there would be on this planet if people would just talk through a problem instead of using violence.

Goal: Do you have a friend or family member you have a really hard time getting through to? Maybe now is the time to try again. It never hurts to try.

August 11

So the moral of the story is, who are you to judge?

—SALT-N-PEPA, "NONE OF YOUR BUSINESS"

Don't waste your time judging other people, it's not your place. You weren't put here to judge others. You are here to be the best version of yourself that you can be and to spread love and kindness to everyone you meet.

Goal: Do not judge other people, use your time making a difference.

If we are to live together in peace we must know each other better.

—LYNDON JOHNSON

We all share space on this planet, so we have to come to a place of mutual respect so we can get along. We don't all have to agree with each other but we have to respect and honor our differences and similarities alike.

Goal: Reach out to your colleague, roommate, coworker, or new acquaintance and make an effort to get to know them a little better. You might be surprised how much you have in common or how touched they are by your effort.

Those who cause suffering are often the ones suffering the most.

When I was bullied as a teenager, I felt a lot of anger about the way people treated me. Now I understand that those people were suffering as much as I was but expressing it in different ways. When I think about the bullies today, it may sound crazy, but I want to hug them because I know they were in need of love and compassion at that time.

Goal: Think about one person today who has hurt you in the past. Have compassion, for they were obviously in pain themselves.

You teach people how to treat you
by what you allow, what you stop,
and what you reinforce.

—TONY GASKINS

If you're an outgoing person, it's important to remember that not everyone is that way. We should all be sensitive to others and what they're comfortable with. Be cautious of other people's boundaries. If anyone starts to cross yours, tell them to please respect them. There have been anxious times in my life where people are trying to pull at me, and I've had to set boundaries or walk away from situations.

Goal: Be aware and considerate of other people's boundaries. Just because you are comfortable acting a certain way, doesn't mean another person is okay with it.

August 15

Have compassion for all beings, rich and poor alike; each has their suffering. Some suffer too much, others too little.

—BUDDHA

Oftentimes when we compare our struggles to others', we end up feeling guilty and accidentally invalidate our own feelings. When I broke my ankle, it really sucked, but I realized someone on the other side of the world may not even have fresh water. Sometimes we instantly shame ourselves because someone is in more pain than we are, but all pain needs to be acknowledged because it's real. And just because you haven't had as much as another doesn't mean you haven't struggled.

Goal: Whatever you are going through, make sure you validate how you are feeling. Value and respect your emotions as if they were someone else's.

August 16

Don't compare yourself to anyone else, you are doing yourself the greatest disservice.

No two people are alike—that is what makes each and every one of us so magnificent and special. It's human nature to judge ourselves, to judge others, and when we're feeling insecure we start comparing ourselves to other people. We think about whether someone has more money than we do, whether someone is prettier or more talented than we are. But it just doesn't matter because that person isn't you and they never will be. You were created exactly as you were meant to be.

Goal: Remember, there is nobody else on this earth who has the heart that you have, and that itself is worth treasuring.

Let every feeling happen to you
Beauty and terror
Just keep going
No feeling is final.

—RAINER MARIA RILKE

When we are deep in one particular feeling we often think it will last forever. The trick is not resisting that emotion because that just causes more pain and suffering. We are here on this earth to feel a range of emotions: beauty and terror, sorrow and bliss, laughter and sadness. You can't control every emotion you go through so it's important to just let the experiences happen knowing that they won't last forever.

Goal: Remember, pain is a part of life. It helps us appreciate the happier times.

August 18

Either you run the day or the day runs you.

—JIM ROHN

When you wake up in a bad mood it seems to always color your day and if you don't catch it in time you will start to feel like your whole day is doomed. Believe it or not, you have the power to change your mood and decide to not let one bad thought or feeling ruin your whole day. I'm not saying it's always easy because I know it can be tough. Give it a try and see what kind of positivity and light you can bring in.

Goal: Exercise the laws of attraction today. No matter what happens to you, keep sending out good energy to the universe and see what it brings back for you.

Do small things with great love.

——MOTHER TERESA

As long as you do everything in your life with all your heart your impact will be more profound than you could ever imagine.

Goal: Even the smaller tasks in life deserve all your heart. Something as simple as a hug or saying "thank you" should be given the same level of love and care as bigger actions.

August 20

Even miracles take time.

——Cinderella

As children we believed that wishes could come true with the flick of a wand or the snap of a finger. It's not to say that wonderful things can't happen quickly, but more often than not, miraculous things take time. I truly believe that miracles can happen. With that faith I am provided with the strength to continue to stay strong.

Goal: Have patience. Even the great changes in our lives need time to occur.

August 21

You don't owe anybody the present other than yourself. Take time for you. Respect yourself and your privacy. Set boundaries.

So many of the lessons I've learned have been about standing up for myself and setting boundaries. It's really hard and sometimes even painful. In work environments and everyday life, be sure to set boundaries for those you're spending time with. Make sure they're aware with what you're comfortable with and your limitations. Take action and communicate with others to make sure you are honoring yourself. It's hard, but it's worth it.

Goal: Set one boundary today in your professional or personal life.

August 22

Thanks to my mother I haven't wasted
any time dwelling on whether I'm
brilliant or a fool. It's completely
unprofitable to think about it.

—WOODY ALLEN

You could spend your entire lifetime worrying what other people think of you but then you would have wasted all your life's energy doing nothing but worrying about things that you have no control over. It really doesn't matter what others think of you. You can't be liked by everybody and that's not why we were put on this earth. What matters is that you can go to sleep at night knowing you did your best and acted with kindness, honesty, and compassion for others and for yourself.

Goal: Spend your days wisely, focus on what matters, not on silly things you can't control, or they will end up controlling you.

Find your purpose, find your voice.

We're all here on this earth for a reason. Some of us know when we are very young what we want to become, and some of us may need more time to discover themselves. No matter when you discover your future, you have a specific purpose on this earth. Your voice is unique and beautiful. When you find out what makes you happy, embrace it and never let anyone tell you that you can't live your dreams.

Goal: List everything you want to accomplish in life. It doesn't matter how big the dream sounds, the bigger the better.

August 24

Live with no regrets.

—UNKNOWN

Nobody is perfect. Equally important is knowing how to forgive yourself. Do not obsess over your past mistakes. The more you obsess and hold on to it, the more energy and power you give it. So let it go, learn from it, and move on.

Goal: Forgive yourself for a mistake you made or something you've done that you now regret. Allow yourself to let it go.

August 25

In the end only three things matter:
how much you loved, how gently you
lived, and how gracefully you let go
of things not meant for you.

—BUDDHA

Why is it that we spend more time obsessing about the one thing that we didn't get instead of all the wonderful things in our lives? Consider the possibility that the one thing you wanted so badly that slipped away just wasn't meant for you. Instead look around and be grateful for all the love and blessings you have right now.

Goal: Think about something you really wanted but never got that turned out to be a blessing in disguise.

August 26

When you do your best and live out your dreams, you inspire others to do the same.

The more energy you spend living your dreams, the more that energy will spread to other people. Your courage to live your dreams will give people courage, inspiration, and freedom to start living out their own dreams. You're a living example of what some people feel is impossible. There's no greater gift you could give someone like that.

Goal: If you're feeling fearful or uninspired about your dreams, spend time with a friend who is motivated and draw inspiration.

Hold faithfulness and sincerity as first principles.

—CONFUCIUS

Sincerity and faithfulness are two of the most fundamental values in life. Without these ideals the world loses its meaning. Every day I try my best to be genuine to myself, my friends, my family, and my fans.

Goal: What are your values? Make sure your daily actions align with your morals and belief system.

August 28

You will never do anything in this world
without courage. It is the greatest quality
of the mind next to honor.

—ARISTOTLE

We don't give ourselves enough credit for all the courage we have
inside ourselves. Perhaps some have more than others, but at the
end of the day, even if you tried and failed, you have already won.
You tried and that takes more courage than anything else.

Goal: Do your very best in everything you do today.

You can spend minutes, hours, days, weeks, or even months overanalyzing a situation, trying to put the pieces together, justifying what could've, would've happened . . . or you can just leave the pieces on the floor and move on.

—TUPAC

If you spend your thoughts and days living in the past, you will find you aren't happy because you're missing out on all the joy and wonder in the present. Zone in on this moment right now. Focus on your breathing and be thankful for where you are. We tend to look in the past and future when our joy is actually right under our nose.

Goal: If you spend too much time living in the past, you aren't able to live in the now. Make an effort to move forward today.

August 30

Your time is limited, so don't waste it on living someone else's life.

—STEVE JOBS

As I started gaining success as an artist I would use the level of that success to measure my own happiness. But as I continued on this path I realized that there were so many ups and downs. I would never be happy with myself if I allowed other people's perceptions and opinions to define who I am. I'm so thankful that I have the strength and self-love to handle my highs and lows.

Goal: Find YOUR strength in self-love. And don't let other people's opinions define you.

August 31

Give what you want to receive. If you want happiness, make others happy.

——RUSSELL SIMMONS

It's a simple law of attraction that you get back what you put out into the universe. The more love you give, the more love you attract. The more love you attract, the more love you receive. When we put good energy into the world, we feel good. We make those around us feel good.

Goal: Be a shining example of every value and ideal you hold dear to your heart.

September

September 1

I'm worthy enough, beautiful enough, and I don't need anything else to feel whole.

—UNKNOWN

When we truly feel whole inside is when we own our beauty and inner strength. Each of us has our own standards for what makes us happy and how we want to live our lives. Those standards are formed and shaped by our own experiences through trial and error. We are meant to constantly evolve and adjust these standards as we change and grow. When you stay true to your voice and your deepest self you will always be whole.

Goal: Today, keep in mind that you don't need anyone else to complete you because you complete yourself.

Love makes your soul crawl out
from its hiding place.

—ZORA NEALE HURSTON

Gossip, judgments, bullying, and other negative influences can make us want to hide our true feelings, whether feelings of sadness, joy, or love. It's not easy to trust that you can be yourself, even with those who love you. When you let in the love of your family and your friends, your heart and soul will soar.

Goal: Take the time to appreciate those who love and support you and accept you for who you are.

September 3

Yesterday is history, tomorrow is a mystery, but today is a gift.

——A. A. MILNE

Nobody knows how long we are on earth for; you don't want to waste your time here stressing about the next day. You should just appreciate the moment and try to cherish it as often as you can.

Goal: Realize that time is limited and challenge yourself to live each day to the fullest. What is a way you can live your life to the fullest today?

September 4

They can lock me up but my spirit and my love can never be confined to prison walls.

—LIL WAYNE

At the end of the day your spirit and soul can never be compromised. No matter what kind of limitations or boundaries people may try to create around you, it's your ability to love yourself and others that moves mountains.

Goal: Don't allow your emotional restrictions to hold you back.

September 5

Life is beautiful . . . You are worthy of it.

Never devalue yourself. *Never* forget how beautiful you really are. People in certain situations can sometimes make us feel we aren't good enough by society's standards. But it's natural to feel that way. You just need to know how to find your way out of that negative place.

Goal: Remind yourself that you are beautiful exactly the way you are.

September 6

Each morning, we are born again. What we do today is what matters most.

—BUDDHA

We're never doomed because we're being reborn each day and life is filled with new opportunities. You have the freedom to wake up one day and decide to travel the world, change career paths, or reach out to a friend you haven't spoken to in years. Every day is filled with new ideas and possibilities.

Goal: Do something unexpected and out of character today. Free yourself.

September 7

Walk by faith, not by sight.

—2 CORINTHIANS 5:7

If I had allowed myself to live and dream based only on what I was seeing right in front of me, I wouldn't be anywhere close to where I am today. But I had faith in my dreams, my imagination, the power of my thoughts, and my hopes for a better life. I could've let the way I was treated in school—the bullying, the mean words said to me—define the way I lived, but I didn't. Rather than choosing the life that was right there in front of me, I had faith that my dreams would carry me through the hard times and ultimately bring me to the place I wanted to get to.

Goal: What is your biggest dream? Speak it out loud and tell yourself that it is right in front of you as long as you believe in it and believe in yourself.

September 8

One of the reasons I was so unhappy for years is that I never embraced my emotions and I was trying to stay in control.

I didn't realize at the time that in my desperate attempt to stay in control of my life I was losing more and more of myself in the process. My addictions gave me a false sense of control. I was in too deep to understand that each day I was getting farther and farther away from myself. I was holding on to so much pain and using my addictions to numb my suffering. When I first got help I felt completely out of control because I no longer had anything to hide behind and I hated that feeling. I didn't understand that I needed to surrender my power to something bigger. I am so thankful today that I let everything out and asked for the help that I needed.

Goal: When someone asks how you are, don't say fine—tell them how you really feel.

September 9

I don't know the key to success, but the key to failure is trying to please everybody.

—BILL COSBY

Oftentimes when you try to please other people you only make them happy and you end up disappointed, whether you realize it or not. If you're young and coming into your age or older and secure in who you are, don't alter who you are for anybody.

Goal: Live life for yourself and everything else will fall into place when the time is right.

September 10

Do something wonderful;
people may imitate it.

—ALBERT SCHWEITZER

Good deeds are contagious, but for some reason, people sometimes need permission. Some people may be afraid to step out of their comfort zones and do something they would feel uncomfortable doing. It's important to set a good example for those around you because other people will follow suit.

Goal: Lead and inspire others with your good deeds.

September 11

If you and I are having a single thought of violence or hatred against anyone in the world at this moment, we are contributing to the wounding of the world.

—DEEPAK CHOPRA

Violence is the easy way out and it only leads to more violence. We need people in this world who are willing to find solutions through peace, through communication, honesty, and diplomacy. World peace may seem impossible, but it's worth aiming for.

Goal: You don't have to be a politician to stop wars and practice peace. Make sure every word you speak and every action is coming from a place of love.

September 12

Even if you're right, the other person still has their side of the story.

No matter how confident you are that you're "right" in a situation, there's a good chance that the person you are in a fight or disagreement with feels equally confident that they're right. Often the reason fights become so complicated is because there isn't just one right answer or solution. It's two-sided and important to listen to all sides before anyone comes to a decision.

Goal: Stay open-minded and be willing to hear the other person's side. They may point something out to you that you never would have thought about that will help you grow.

September 13

If you don't want to slip up tomorrow, speak the truth today.

—BRUCE LEE

Each one of us has told countless lies, big and small—I suppose it's human. Even if you tell just the smallest lie, be direct with yourself right away, come clean, and apologize.

Goal: Do not tell a single lie today no matter how small.

There's nothing more beautiful and attractive than a person who knows who they are.

It's so attractive when someone just knows exactly who they are and doesn't compromise it. When a man or a woman walks into a room and has confidence, everyone can feel it. The truth is that looks fade, but inner beauty, poise, and self-love last forever—but only if you nurture them.

Goal: Find your confidence and let it radiate out.

September 15

What other people think of me
is none of my business.

——ANONYMOUS

You could spend all of your days obsessing over what other people think of you and at some point or another we have all gone down this road. Everyone has an opinion but it doesn't really matter because other people's opinions shouldn't affect what you are doing with your life. Your business is your business. The moment you begin to let other people's thoughts and values start dictating how you live your own life, it is no longer yours.

Goal: Take constructive criticism but don't let anyone's opinions change you.

September 16

You are who your friends are.

I learned that the people I was surrounding myself with were direct reflections of me. I found that if they were using drugs while I was sober, a tiny part of me wanted to be friends with them because they were using. I had to learn that I couldn't be friends with people who are still active in their disease. I've had to cut people out of my life because they were bringing me down. Now that I am in recovery I make it a point to surround myself with positive people who have integrity and strong values.

Goal: What matters to you most in a friend? Write down your values and virtues and make sure that the people you surround yourself with meet those criteria.

September 17

You don't need to look like everybody else.
Love who you are.

——LEA MICHELE

No matter who we are, we all have days when we feel insecure.
The most important thing is to know we all have days like this.
It's only when we accept that emotion that we're able to feel it
and move on with our day.

Goal: When you feel insecure—look in the mirror and give
yourself positive affirmations.

September 18

Nothing will work unless you do.

——MAYA ANGELOU

In order to bring the highest version of yourself to everything you do, you must be performing at your highest level. That means making sure you get enough sleep, eat well, exercise, meditate, and take care of your mind, body, and soul. Sometimes we think we have to show how hard we work by burning ourselves out, but I promise you it's so much better to find the balance. You will feel happier, you will be more productive, and your work will be better.

Goal: Look at your life and find balance in all aspects and areas.

September 19

Expectations are just disappointments waiting to happen.

When we spend our time waiting for things to happen we aren't living in the now and we set ourselves up to be let down and end up judging ourselves, which only makes us feel worse. It's important to know what you want for your life. At the same time it's also important to be open to how and where those dreams will be fulfilled. The problematic thing about expectation is that it builds our hopes up too high. It's wonderful to be a dreamer but it's also important to be grounded and realistic.

Goal: Release your expectations, stay open to the journey, and explore what is right in front of you.

And all the colors I am inside
have not been invented yet.

——SHEL SILVERSTEIN

Creativity is so much more than just producing art. It also allows you to purge toxic emotions and thoughts in a positive, healthy way. For me, it's singing and playing music. When I perform, I'm able to express my emotions without engaging in self-destructive behaviors.

Goal: Find a hobby that allows you to release strong emotions in a healthy way.

September 21

Remember not getting what you want is sometimes a wonderful stroke of luck.

—ANONYMOUS

So many times in life I didn't get something I wanted, something I thought was perfect for me. I see now that those things I thought I needed were exactly what I didn't need. Even if you can't understand it now, be humble about letting those disappointments go and accept that it may be for the best.

Goal: Reflect on initial disappointments and how they turned out to be blessings.

We are always the same age inside.

—GERTRUDE STEIN

Remember how amazing it felt to be a little kid? Running around outside and playing with your friends without a care in the world? Just because we grow up doesn't mean we have to lose our inner child. That little girl or boy is still inside you. They don't get to call the shots anymore, but they should still be able to play and experience pure joy.

Goal: Remember to find enjoyment in your work and find fun in everything you do.

September 23

You are the only person in this world
who knows how to live your life.

If someone tells you otherwise then they are struggling with living their own life and they've decided it's easier to tell other people what to do. They are afraid of their own reality, but you can help by showing them how you live life fearlessly and with conviction.

Goal: Embrace your life today exactly as it is, with all its flaws and perfections, its hopes and disappointments. Inspire others to live their lives more presently and more fully, by showing them the faith and confidence you have in the life YOU are living. Lead by example.

At times our own light goes out and is
rekindled by a spark from another person.
Each of us has cause to think with deep
gratitude of those who have lighted
the flame within us.

—ALBERT SCHWEITZER

We can't be positive and optimistic every day of the year—it's only natural. Sometimes our light is as bright as the sun, and sometimes it can be a little faint. It's important to surround yourself with friends who love unconditionally. These are the people we look to when we feel that all hope is lost. True friends light up our lives and rekindle the light within us when our hope is weakened.

Goal: If you're having a bad day, surround yourself with friends who will let their light shine over you.

September 25

What examples are we setting for our younger brothers, sisters, and children? Start changing their future today.

I have a little sister whom I love with all my heart. Regardless of whether or not I was in the spotlight, I would really be thinking about how my own actions might influence my little sister in her life. If I'm doing drugs in front of her, she's going to think that's okay. We have to be conscious and mindful of all the things that we do and say knowing that younger generations are looking up to us.

Goal: Set a good example for the influential people in your life.

There is always an opportunity to turn a
negative situation into a positive one as long
as you are open to the possibility.

Every difficult situation I've experienced has ultimately changed
me for the better. I've grown stronger as an artist and a human
being and I have been able to advocate for others who are still
struggling to be heard. I can't tell you what a privilege and an
honor it is for me to use my own pain to help people find strength
and hopefully prevent unneeded suffering for many others. These
positive rays of light were only able to come through the darkness
because I allowed them to, because I was open to them, and
because I didn't dwell on my past or my pain—I simply honored it.

Goal: Find something positive about a struggle you're facing
and share it with someone who's struggling. They'll know something better is coming to them too.

We are afraid to care too much for fear that
the other person doesn't care at all.

—ELEANOR ROOSEVELT

Never be afraid to show someone how much you love them.
There have been many times in my life when I have wanted to
tell someone how much I loved them, but I was afraid I'd seem
uncool. When I got over that and realized how grateful they
were for my expression of love, they gave it right back to me. It
took my openness to help them open up.

Goal: Be open with someone in your life and encourage them
to do the same.

September 28

Be impeccable with your word.

—MIGUEL ANGEL RUIZ

It's so important to say what you mean in life. Sometimes we are afraid to say something that'll hurt or disappoint someone. But real pain and disappointment are caused when we say something that we don't mean or make a promise that we can't fulfill. Over the years I too have promised things I couldn't deliver and said things I later regretted. I wanted to believe that I could but deep down I knew it wasn't realistic for me. Make sure you're speaking words you can stand by. Even if you feel like you aren't promising enough, at least you know you'll have been honest.

Goal: Stay accountable for your actions. Everything you say today should come from a place of honesty and truth.

Don't procrastinate happiness.

There was a time when I was so down and depressed. All I wanted was to feel happiness and I constantly looked for it outside of myself. I heard the expression "Change your thoughts, change your life." At first I wasn't sure about it because I blamed external forces and other people for my unhappiness. I decided to try changing my thoughts and I found that I was instantly a happier person. The power of the mind is so incredible; when I started being proactive about leading a happy life it made all the difference.

Goal: Happiness may come tomorrow, but don't rely on that. Get on your road to happiness today and now.

Be bold and mighty;
forces will come to your aid.

—GOETHE

When you know what you want in life all that matters is that you go after it with conviction and courage. You don't have to know every little step in order to achieve your dream.

Goal: Take a bold step toward the unknown and trust that the ground will appear beneath you when you need it.

October

October 1

We can't control all in life . . . but what we can do is look ahead and dictate where we go next.

Life will bring you every kind of emotion and experience you can think of, and plenty that you'd never even imagine. I try to take everything that comes to me with gratitude. Life is about not knowing and making the best of any situation.

Goal: Think about something wonderful that lies ahead for you.

October 2

Don't worry, be happy.

—BOBBY MCFERRIN, "DON'T WORRY, BE HAPPY"

It's a pretty simple concept yet it can be so difficult to just stop worrying. Worrying doesn't do anything but suspend our happiness. It works, so give it a shot and see if your mood improves.

Goal: Listen to a happy, upbeat song to get you back on track.

October 3

When you hate, the only person that suffers
is you because most of the people you hate
don't know it and the rest don't care.

——MEDGAR EVERS

Whenever I was getting over a breakup I used to spend most of
my time filled with anger and hate. I didn't realize it then, but I
had so much toxicity in my life. I always wondered why my exes
were able to get over the breakup faster than I was. Now I realize
it was because I was spending so much time hating them rather
than getting over it. Similarly when I was twelve and I was being
bullied, I spent more time angry at my bullies instead of just taking the time to be loving and nurturing to myself.

Goal: Whatever struggle you are facing in your life, make sure
you are not poisoning yourself with anger when you could be
giving yourself love.

October 4

The most valuable possession you can own is an open heart.

——CARLOS SANTANA

You never know from which direction something wonderful will come into your life. You might be so set on one thing in your mind but the universe has something else even more wonderful in store for you. If you are only looking in one direction you might miss it. It's important to be focused on your dreams and visions but at the same time stay open to any and all possibilities.

Goal: Do something today you wouldn't normally do, and see what it feels like. You might enjoy a new part of life.

October 5

We cannot start over but we can start now
and make a new ending.

—ZIG ZIGLAR

Allow all of your hopes, dreams, and visions for your life to fill
up your heart, energize, and inform every word you speak, and
give new meaning to every step you take.

Goal: Be fearless, ambitious, brave, and courageous in your
personal and professional life.

October 6

The simple things are also the most
extraordinary things, and only
the wise can see them.

——PAULO COELHO

When was the last time you observed the world around you?
There are so many small moments to notice in this life. Don't
become completely wrapped up in your own world that you stop
noticing everything else.

Goal: Take in as many little moments and details as you can.

Proud people breed sad sorrows
for themselves.

——EMILY BRONTË

I think many of us have had a moment where we were too proud to either ask for help or say I don't know. Pride can hinder us and our ability to learn. Never be ashamed or embarrassed to ask for help or say you don't know or understand something.

Goal: Ask lots of questions about the things you don't understand. You're not weak, you're just expanding your mind by learning.

Promises are like the full moon, if they are not kept at once, they diminish day by day.

——GERMAN PROVERB

It's easy for us to say we'll take action, but if we don't follow through with it then we're just making empty promises. If you can't follow through with the promises that you make, especially to yourself, then you will not only hurt others but you will damage your integrity.

Goal: If you have hurt someone recently by not following through with a promise, make amends with them by apologizing.

There is only one way to avoid criticism: say nothing, be nothing, do nothing.

—ARISTOTLE

You can't please everyone and you're not supposed to. I've taken a lot of criticism and even read horrible comments on the Internet, but I can't let that bring me down. I have to keep being who I am for the people in my life that matter and that will be enough.

Goal: Don't try to please everyone, just focus on pleasing yourself. If someone is over-criticizing you, don't feed into them by responding.

October 10

Ego is a social fiction for which one person at a time gets all the blame.

—ROBERT ANTON WILSON

We are not our egos and we cannot blame everything on our egos. We have to take responsibility for the decisions we make in life even if that means putting our personal feelings aside and doing what's right. Even though it may not be easy on our pride.

Goal: Let go of your ego and take responsibility for your actions.

Respond intelligently even to unintelligent treatment.

—LAO TZU

There will be people in life who'll say things to bring you down to their level. But we all have a choice about how we deal with that kind of treatment. It's really hard to not react when all you want to do is make them feel as bad as they've made you feel. But I promise you that's never the answer. Be patient and take the time to respond with grace, not for the sake of the other person but for yourself.

Goal: The next time someone treats you poorly, do not reciprocate. Be the bigger person with your response.

October 12

The struggles and the chaos are part of life.
But you have to accept them with grace
and serenity because they have
their own gifts too.

All my struggles and the journey I have taken have been a tremendous gift. They have allowed me to grow as an artist and a
human being. Once I started accepting the struggles and decided
to learn from them (instead of them controlling me), I felt so
much more at ease. Now I realize that these struggles and challenges have actually helped me grow as an artist and a woman.

Goal: When you're consumed in chaos, remember that many
positive changes will follow.

Keep away from people who belittle
your ambitions. Small people always do
that, but the really great make you
feel that you, too, can become great.

—MARK TWAIN

I've had to learn the hard way who my real friends are, but the best way for me to tell is if they want to lift me up or bring me down. I only want to be with people who support me and in turn make me feel stronger because of their love and belief in me and because of my love and belief in them. You can't have a friendship that's one-sided—you have to get as much as you give.

Goal: It might be worth letting a toxic person in your life know how you feel. If they aren't willing to change the way they treat you, consider not spending so much time with them.

October 14

A Wounded Deer—leaps the highest—

—EMILY DICKINSON

Our wounds and scars give us strength and courage. Mine have made every moment in life more meaningful, and in the end I know myself better. I'm stronger and my passion for life is deeper. I can finally appreciate my wounds for the blessings that they brought me.

Goal: Embrace your past difficulties and painful experiences—they helped shape you. You are stronger for having gone through all that you have, and no matter what, you stand here today able to talk about them.

October 15

God didn't do it all in one day.
What makes you think you can?

——UNKNOWN

No matter how hard you work it's really important to take breaks. Stand up, stretch your muscles, have a five-minute meditation, and quiet your mind. When you go back to whatever you'e doing you will be more productive. When I spend a sixteen-hour day at the studio it's so easy to lose myself in my work because I love what I'm doing. It's really important that I stand up and get some air. It makes me feel better and keeps my work fresh.

Goal: Recharge your battery by taking a moment for yourself each day.

October 16

Words have the power to both destroy
and heal. When words are both true and
kind, they can change our world.

—BUDDHA

There is so much power in our words—more than we realize.
They can do so much good and so much damage. They can create peace or cause people to break out in violence. When we're
hurting the most it's easy to lash out at other people, but then we
become the source of the problem we are personally suffering
from. Don't take your pain out on others or you will just be per-
petuating the cycle.

Goal: If you're hurting, do your best to seek outlets that are
healthy. Find a friend to talk to, express yourself artistically,
write in your journal, or seek professional help.

October 17

The practice of forgiveness is our most important contribution to the healing of the world.

——MARIANNE WILLIAMSON

If everyone in the world were to hold on to all their past resent-
ments and cling to their pain, there would be no hope for the
future because everyone would be angry and bitter, glued to
their past. The practice of forgiveness is powerful beyond words.
Forgiveness is an infectiously beautiful act of humility. It means
you are able to put aside your ego and decide that it's better to be
happy and at peace than to be "right."

Goal: Invest your energy in things that make you happy and
don't worry about being right.

October 18

Never give up.

We've all heard this phrase countless times in our lives. It's only through living this motto that I've come to understand why so many clichéd phrases are so truthful. Sometimes when your dreams and your faith are challenged it's not that all hope is lost. Instead it means you're being tested. When you rise above the challenges and show the universe that you want it in spite of everything, your prayers will be answered and your dreams will be fulfilled.

Goal: Think about what it is you really love doing in this life and keep chasing it.

October 19

People often say that motivation doesn't
last. Well, neither does bathing—
that's why we recommend it daily.

—ZIG ZIGLAR

Just remember: Whatever goals you are working on right now,
you have to work at them every day. It's not enough just to write
out your goals and visions for the future; you have to work hard
to get anything in life.

Goal: Make a point to spend every day of this month doing at
least one thing to bring you closer to your goal.

October 20

If we wait for the moment when
everything, absolutely everything is
ready, we shall never begin.

—IVAN TURGENEV

Don't sit around and wait for the timing to be just right. There's
no such thing as a perfectly opportune moment. Had I waited for
the perfect moment to start my career, I wouldn't be where I am
today. So work hard and dream big. You just have to go out there
and make it happen for yourself.

Goal: Stop procrastinating a goal you have.

Nothing is a waste of time if you use the experience wisely.

—RODIN

So much of my journey and life has been about figuring out who I am. I used to think that if I didn't already know everything then I never would. Now I've come to realize that it's the process and the journey that have defined me and made me whole. It's taking risks, trying new things, and continuing to grow and learn that matter the most. I know I'm being guided toward it, and that's enough. I want to keep growing, keep learning, and exploring. Embrace the unknown because that's where all the magic lies.

Goal: Be grateful for your journey because it is yours alone.

October 22

When we love, we always strive to become better than we are. When we strive to become better than we are, everything around us becomes better too.

—PAULO COELHO

Love is the ultimate healer, the best remedy. Love makes all things possible. It empowers us and allows us to become more open and compassionate than we ever dreamed. There is no such thing as loving too much. People will be grateful that you are able to love with all your heart.

Goal: Use your love and the love from others to heal yourself.

October 23

So starting today, I'm breaking out of this cage.

—EMINEM, "NOT AFRAID"

Whatever you have been through in life there's always an opportunity to break out, to break through your struggles. Many of us have to experience something really horrible before we can get to the other side. Regardless of where you are at this moment, don't forget that it gets better and that you always have a choice to ask for help and face your demons.

Goal: Look inside yourself, gather all your strenth, and stare down what's holding you back.

October 24

Twenty years from now you will be more disappointed by the things you didn't do than by the ones you did do. So throw off the bowlines. Sail away from the safe harbor. Catch the trade winds in your sails. Explore. Dream. Discover.

——MARK TWAIN

As an artist, you have to be fearless about pursuing your dreams. You have to be willing to leave your comfort zone to grow not only as a human being but to push your own boundaries. I encourage anyone chasing dreams to be fearless; go into emotional areas that aren't always comfortable or comprehensible.

Goal: Do something out of your comfort zone today. Sometimes the things that scare us help us grow.

October 25

Never expect, never assume, never ask,
and never demand. Just let it be. Because
if it is meant to be, it will happen.

When we learn that we can only control our actions in this life, it seems confining and even unsettling because on some level we all want to feel like we're in complete control. But when I thought more about this I came to a deeper understanding that actually made me feel free. Some things may happen exactly as you planned and others may not, but in the end it will be exactly as it should be.

Goal: Think about one thing in life you have no control over right now and find peace in that.

October 26

When anger rises, your conscience falls,
so be aware of your self-righteousness
and try to see it from all points of view.

Anger is such a powerful emotion, so much so that when we really experience it, it has the tendency to cloud our judgment and our ability to reason. We have to accept our feelings but also know that when we don't regulate our anger it has the ability to destroy our common sense.

Goal: Don't let your anger get the best of you. Think rationally and be careful of how your emotions affect others.

October 27

We can't change the world unless
we change ourselves.

—BIGGIE SMALLS

As imperfect beings on this earth it's important to always stay open, to keep growing and expanding. When we change ourselves and seek to improve our lives we make the world a better place.

Goal: Join a philanthropic cause—do your part in the world.

October 28

You can't live your life for other people.
You've got to do what's right for you, even
if it hurts some people you love.

——NICHOLAS SPARKS

Celebrate your independence today and the fact that you can
make your own decisions. It's impossible to please everybody
around you but it is always possible to make the right choices to
please yourself. In the end that's all you can worry about.

Goal: Don't make decisions based on other peoples influences
or advice.

October 29

I still believe, in spite of everything,
that people are truly good at heart.

—ANNE FRANK

If Anne Frank, who went through such unimaginable trauma, could still maintain a positive attitude and believe in the goodness of others, then I can too.

Goal: When you're feeling sorry for yourself or need perspective—think of how good your life actually is. You are blessed.

October 30

Keep your face to the sunshine and you cannot see a shadow.

—HELEN KELLER

The fact that this quote came from someone who couldn't even see is so profoundly beautiful. She was able to see the light within herself and within each of us just by shifting her perspective; this attitude is so admirable and something we can all learn from.

Goal: Choose to surround yourself with positivity and you will be able to handle any challenges.

One of the scariest things in life is when you come to the realization that the only thing that can save you is . . . yourself.

There came a time, after treatment, when I realized no matter how many people I leaned on, nobody was going to save me unless I saved myself. Change comes from within, not from other people. You can't force someone to change.

Goal: Look inside yourself and honestly answer the question, do I need guidance?

November

You have to stand up for yourself because nobody else will.

There have been times in my life when I knew there was something wrong about the way I was being treated but I was too afraid or shy to stand up for myself. It can be really hard and scary for people, because I think we're afraid that we will be liked less. But if you don't stand up for what you believe in, then you will get taken advantage of. Whether it's intentional or unintentional, it feels just as awful. I believe that when you start standing up for yourself, you will actually be respected so much more.

Goal: Stand up for yourself with grace and confidence; own your power.

November 2

Love yourself today 'cause, baby, you were born this way.

—LADY GAGA, "BORN THIS WAY"

Often when you're bullied or teased, it will have negative and lasting effects. When I was younger, I was losing my identity because I was changing things about myself the bullies didn't like. One day, I realized I was no longer myself. I needed to love who I was and who I'd always been. Once I found that, I was able to feel better about myself.

Goal: Never sacrifice yourself by trying to conform to other people's standards.

November 3

Be kind to unkind people,
they need it the most.

—ASHLEIGH BRILLIANT

When you start observing strangers you will find that some people seem truly happy while others seem like they're angry at the world. Don't take it personally because those people are suffering on the inside. Think about the miserable-looking guy in line next to you or the security guy at the airport yelling at everyone; those people are obviously yelling because of something negative they are feeling on the inside. They need kindness the most and they will most likely be extremely touched you reached out even if they don't know how to show it. If you're vulnerable with them, they will most likely be vulnerable with you.

Goal: Today, respond to anger in a positive manner.

November 4

This is a good sign, having a broken heart;
it means we have tried for something.

——ELIZABETH GILBERT

There will always be times when we try genuinely for something and end up feeling disappointed. It means that you were willing to take a risk. Even though the pain can hurt I hope you remember that it's a good sign because it shows you care. It's a reflection of all the love you have inside of you.

Goal: Love fearlessly and bravely with all your heart.

November 5

Nobody deserves your tears, but whoever deserves them will not make you cry.

—GABRIEL GARCÍA MÁRQUEZ

There will be plenty of people who will bring you to tears in life or at least make you feel like you want to cry. Those people do not deserve your tears. The people who will be there to comfort you when you cry and help you wipe them away are the ones who will never make you feel that way.

Goal: Do your best to surround yourself with people who will comfort you and help lift you up when times are hard.

November 6

We should regret our mistakes and
learn from them, but never carry them
forward into the future with us.

—L. M. MONTGOMERY

We already know that no one is perfect, but knowing that doesn't
keep us from doing things we might feel badly about later. I've
found in times like that it's best to come clean and own your mistake. People will be so much more forgiving and sympathetic
when you are honest about it because they can relate. Even better, you will inspire them to do the same thing by showing them
how honest and beautiful you can be without being perfect.

Goal: Tell on yourself today about something you feel badly
about having done or said in the past month.

November 7

Honestly have you ever been honest with yourself.

—TERMINAL, "DARK"

In life we often need to reevaluate where we are and the things that we're feeling. I remember hearing this lyric and thinking, wow, am I being myself right now or just trying to fit in to whatever society wants me to be? It's always helpful to remind yourself to always stay true to who you really are.

Goal: Discover yourself and don't compromise your values.

November 8

I dream of painting and then
I paint my dream.

—VINCENT VAN GOGH

Your dreams are amazing gifts. All my life I dreamed about being a performer. I wanted to sing, dance, and act. Those dreams allowed me to go after what I really wanted. Now that I've acted on my dreams, I'm thankful for where I am today.

Goal: Work hard to achieve your dreams and goals. Only you can bring your dreams to life.

November 9

We all need someone to look up to.

Where I am today . . . I still have my ups and downs, but I take it one day at a time. I just hope that I can be the best that I can possibly be, not only for myself, but also for others. We all need encouraging influences in our lives and it's important to surround ourselves with them.

Goal: Who looks up to you? Make sure you are being a good influence and inspiration by helping others.

November 10

Accept that living in the present moment, with your present desires, is the best, the highest thing you can do.

——DEEPAK CHOPRA

All we can do is take things one day, one moment, at a time. To get too caught up in where we've been or where we're going only takes you off your path. The present is all we have, so in order to honor your existence here on this planet it's important to root yourself firmly to the moment you are in.

Goal: Pull your mind from the past and future. Live in the now.

November 11

When you choose to enjoy the process,
your happiness is no longer reliant
upon an outcome.

—YEHUDA BERG

If you have your heart set on a specific outcome, don't obsess. Outcomes change and vary too much to be exactly what we hope or wish. Just take the time to savor and enjoy the process and trust that the rest will happen when it's supposed to.

Goal: Think back on a time when the process of achieving a goal was better than reaching your actual goal.

November 12

Whatever your practice or passion is, you must exercise discipline.

It's not enough to just love doing something if you want to be good at it. You have to practice every day. Before I perform, go on tour, or record in the studio, I have to practice singing and playing my music. If I just show up on the day unprepared, I won't fulfill the high expectations that I have for myself.

Goal: Take time out of your life to practice your passion. Do whatever you need to do that will propel you toward your goals.

November 13

When you reach the end of your rope, tie a knot in it and hang on.

—FRANKLIN D. ROOSEVELT

When it feels like there's nothing you can do—hold on. In time, something else will show up and present you with another option and you will know what to do. Never give up and let go.

Goal: Have faith in tomorrow even when you don't know what it looks like.

Let your conscience be your guide.

—Pinocchio

Your conscience is an inner feeling or voice that acts as a guide to your behavior. Through the years we've received so many lessons from our parents, teachers, friends, and colleagues. At the end of the day we only have those lessons and our instincts to ultimately tell us what's right for us.

Goal: Clear your mind and conscience by righting your wrongs—no matter how small.

November 15

Life is more fun if you play games.

—ROALD DAHL

More than anything I really believe we are put here on this earth to enjoy the time we have. Life is precious so don't get hung up or bent out of shape over the small stuff. Enjoy the present moment and have fun, whatever that means to you.

Goal: Enjoy free time with family and friends. Enjoy a laugh and make some memories.

November 16

"No" is a complete sentence.

—ANONYMOUS

Just saying "no" is fine. Nobody else in this world but you knows what your boundaries are. If something feels off or wrong, you have to listen to that voice. When you say yes or no that's enough; you don't have to explain yourself. The people you surround yourself with should understand that.

Goal: Don't be afraid to say no. You are not obliged to give any answer or response you don't want to give.

November 17

Not all who wander are lost.

—J. R. R. TOLKIEN

Every road you take will lead you to a destination you were supposed to arrive at. Whether that destination was a dead end or a light at the end of the tunnel, know that you were never lost. You were just meant to learn something from the journey you were on.

Goal: Remember that if you don't have a clear path at the moment, don't worry. It doesn't mean you're drifting, it just means you're going about your journey in a different way.

November 18

Girls will be your friends—they'll act like it anyway. But just remember, some come, some go. The ones that stay with you through everything—they're your true best friends. Don't let go of them.

—MARILYN MONROE

Girls can be really hard on each other. I experienced so much bullying and heartache from girls who teased me. I now know what to look for in my girlfriends and I know when to walk away too. When I'm down or having a rough day or need a shoulder to cry on my truest friends have risen to the top.

Goal: Make a list of your closest girlfriends and call them to tell them how much their friendship, support, and love mean to you.

November 19

Be thankful for what you have; you'll end up having more. If you concentrate on what you don't have, you will never, ever have enough.

—OPRAH WINFREY

When we choose to focus on what we have we are instantly happier people. Gratitude is said to be the emotion that is most connected with happiness. Even the wealthiest person in the world can think of things they don't have. It's not about accumulating more things; it's about focusing on the joy and beauty in your life by focusing on what is great in your life.

Goal: Don't decide happiness based on your material possessions, but on the love in your life today.

November 20

The great enemy of clear language is insincerity.

—GEORGE ORWELL

One of my biggest pet peeves is when I see people not being genuine with others. People can always tell when you're not being sincere and if you're not staying true to yourself, you're only fooling yourself.

Goal: Only speak genuinely and cordially.

Spiritual realization is to see clearly that what I perceive, experience, think, or feel is ultimately not who I am, that I cannot find myself in all those things that continuously pass away.

—ECKHART TOLLE

It's the things we cannot express or grasp that are the truest and hold the most meaning. There's also something humbling and beautiful when there are no words to properly relay how profound something is. We don't always have to find the perfect words.

Goal: Trust in your own ability to feel something and be thankful you have the depth to feel things that you can't always express.

November 22

If I choose to bless another person, I will always end up feeling more blessed.

—MARIANNE WILLIAMSON

Whenever you are feeling sorry for yourself or full of self-loathing, it's always best to do something for others to get out of your own head. When you were a kid there was really no greater feeling than opening up Christmas or birthday presents. But when you get older you realize it's putting a smile on someone else's face that really is the biggest gift of all.

Goal: Spread joy by giving to others.

November 23

Do you not see how necessary a
World of Pains and troubles is to school
an Intelligence and make it a soul?

—— JOHN KEATS

We are here on this earth to experience every emotion under
the sun. This gives us strength, heart, and character. It shapes
who we are today and what sort of person we'll be in future.

Goal: Think about or talk to the people in your life you admire
and ask them what experiences shaped their lives.

November 24

Cherish your visions and your dreams
as they are the children of your soul, the
blueprints of your ultimate achievements.

—NAPOLEON HILL

Ever since I was little I knew I wanted to sing and perform. What I know now that I didn't fully understand as a child was that the visions and dreams I began having at such a young age were paving the way not only for my success, but more importantly, for my happiness. I'm so thankful that I listened to those feelings, dreams, and visions at such a young age.

Goal: No matter how old you are it's never too late to live the life you have always dreamed of.

November 25

I am not fearless. I get scared plenty.
But I have also learned how to channel
that emotion to sharpen me.

——BEAR GRYLLS

All fear has ever done is hold me back. I have so many things I
want to accomplish in my life. For myself and for the world. Fear
is useless; it just gets in the way of accomplishing everything.

Goal: Overcome fear today, and confront one of your phobias.

November 26

I don't think anyone can give you advice when you've got a broken heart.

—BRITNEY SPEARS

No matter what people tell you when your heart is broken, there's nothing that really makes it feel better than time and space. We can't get through heartache without the love of our family and friends, but sometimes there's nothing anyone can do to make it better. There's a difference between feeling supported and feeling like someone's trying to fix you. So when your heart or someone else's heart is broken just remember the most important thing you can do is let it run its course.

Goal: Offer your shoulder to cry on for a friend or family member.

November 27

Kindness is the language which the deaf can hear and the blind can see.

—MARK TWAIN

Kindness transcends the boundaries of language, sickness, or disability. It is a universal human gift we all have to give and receive so don't waste it.

Goal: Be kind to a stranger today.

November 28

Life is too short to not be grateful for
every moment we are alive. Today I
have so much to be thankful for.

Sometimes in life it's easy to focus on what we don't have. It's
imperative to remember to be thankful for all you have. When
you focus on all the beautiful things in your life, you will attract
that in abundance and you connect with the many blessings in
your life. Sometimes when I wake up or before I go to sleep, I
make a list of everything I'm grateful for and before I know it, I
have pages of things and I am smiling and beaming with complete
happiness.

Goal: Make a donation to a charity or volunteer your time this
month to help others less fortunate than yourself.

Everyone has been made for some particular work and the desire for that work has been put in every heart.

—RUMI

We all feel lost at one point or another. Sometimes in order to really understand and know where we want to go, we need to feel lost. No matter what you're feeling, just remember that each and every one of us has been put here with a purpose and a passion. Our only job is to realize and follow it. If you haven't realized it yet, don't feel bad. Trust in the universe that you will when you're meant to and in the meantime stay open and grateful for everything that comes your way.

Goal: Take your time to wander when you're feeling lost. Sooner or later you'll decide which direction to go.

November 30

Love is louder than the pressure
to be perfect.

Don't worry about being perfect. Spend your time and energy making sure that you are spending your life giving and receiving love. Nobody will remember you for your imperfections—they will remember you for your kindness, good humor, and compassion.

Goal: Stop trying to be perfect, and start loving more.

December

December 1

The past is a ghost, the future a dream and all
we have is now.

—BILL COSBY

It never ceases to amaze me how time moves so quickly through
our lives. The older I get, I find that it just goes faster and faster.
When you are a kid, each day seems like it could last forever. It
makes me realize that we have to savor each moment, however
big or small, and every person that comes into our lives.

Goal: Don't let the day pass you by—do something meaningful for yourself or someone else.

December 2

There is only one page left to write on.
I will fill it with words of one syllable.
I love. I have loved. I will love.

—*I Capture the Castle*

You don't have to be a ten-year-old girl to keep a diary or a journal of your life. Keeping a daily record of the things that take place in your life and the way you feel about them is incredibly profound. Not only does it help you come to a deeper understanding of what's going on around you, but it's an incredible thing to look back on as you get older. We always think we'll remember a certain incredible moment in life but if we don't write it down we probably won't. Think about what a cherished treasure it will be for you to read about your life in years to come.

Goal: Start some kind of diary or journal or a place just for you to keep track of your life and your feelings.

December 3

You never know how strong you are until being strong is the only choice you have.

—UNKNOWN

It's the times we are tested in life when we really have the choice to rise to the occasion. When you do, you are all the better for taking on the challenge and letting yourself grow into the strongest character you can be.

Goal: Don't underestimate yourself when handed a tough situation. Be proud of your strength.

December 4

I can be changed by what happens to me.
But I refuse to be reduced by it.

——MAYA ANGELOU

Every experience we go through is there to teach us, to humble us, and to help us grow. There's no experience or person on this earth that should ever make us feel less. What happens in life will invariably change you—but don't let it bring you down. If someone ever makes you feel less because you are learning or growing, then it is only a reflection of their dissatisfaction with themselves.

Goal: Do not let anyone tell you how to feel.

December 5

The eyes are the window to the soul.

—WILLIAM SHAKESPEARE

One of my biggest pet peeves is when I see people talking to other people without looking at the other person in the eyes. We all have so much power when we speak from the heart, but if we don't really look at them when we talk, we won't be able to connect with them. It's often in the eyes where we see how a person is really feeling—not in their words. Body language also speaks volumes, so it's important to be aware of how you're carrying yourself.

Goal: Whomever you speak to, make sure you look them in the eyes and connect with them. They will respect you more, and you will respect yourself more.

December 6

If you're going through hell, keep going.

—WINSTON CHURCHILL

Everyone is entitled to have their bad days—don't take it personally. Having all the wisdom and advice in the world doesn't mean we all won't have the occasional bad day. If someone isn't in the best mood and they're short with you—it's not your fault. Let them cool off. We all have days like that. Take a break and decompress. It'll pass.

Goal: If you're having a bad day, unplug, and relax. Take some time for yourself.

December 7

I'm not perfect and I don't have to be.

When I first realized this I felt an intense relief. This realization allowed me to actually become a better person. It gave me the strength to embrace my flaws and learn from my mistakes. The pressure melted away. I wouldn't have been able to start examining my mistakes if I felt like I had to be perfect. Once I found out it was okay to be imperfect, everything changed for the better.

Goal: Don't criticize yourself for making mistakes—just be conscious not to make the same mistake twice.

December 8

I paint self-portraits because I am so often
alone, because I am the person I know best.

—FRIDA KAHLO

All we can do is be authentic to who we really are, to honor the deepest and truest parts of ourselves. There have been so many moments in my life when the only thing that could truly comfort me was music. Knowing that I could sit alone in my room and create a song to express the way I felt brought me so much comfort. It helped me learn how to love my solitude. I encourage each and every one of you to find the same thing for yourself and nurture it every single day.

Goal: Let the thing you love become your protector and your best friend.

December 9

Now I'm a warrior, I've got thicker skin,
I'm a warrior, I'm stronger than I've ever been,
And my armor is made of steel, you can't get in,
I'm a warrior and you can never hurt me again.

When I wrote these lyrics I had something specific in mind, but they can be applied to anyone who has ever had to go through something painful. This song and its message are so important to me because I meet so many who have dealt with all forms of traumas in their lives and feel ashamed or afraid to stand up for themselves. I wrote this song to inspire people of all ages to know that they are not alone and there is always help.

Whatever you are experiencing it *will* get better.

Goal: We all have our battle wounds. The only way to protect yourself is to show people your strength by protecting and loving yourself.

December 10

Understand that just as it is complicated
to make things simple, it is simple to
make things complicated as well.

It's normal for us to overanalyze and overcomplicate just about
everything. We often lead complex lives where the solutions can
seem out of reach. They say the simplest answer is usually cor-
rect, so when I get overwhelmed, I come back to this profound
notion of simplicity. When in doubt, simplify the clutter of your
mind.

Goal: Imagine your problem is a messy knot and visualize
yourself untying it.

December 11

Judging a person does not define who they are. It defines who you are.

—UNKNOWN

I have been through so much and done so many things I could easily be judged for. I would never want to judge anyone else for whatever paths they are on; it's just not my place to criticize someone else's journey. Nor is it anyone else's place to criticize my own.

Goal: Don't judge others. Think about how you'd want to be treated.

December 12

There are no strangers here; only friends you haven't met yet.

—W. B. YEATS

We live in a global community, which expands more and more each day with the rapid advancements in social media. It's so amazing to wake up to encouraging messages on Twitter and Facebook from my fans all over the world and realize that I have friends and supporters wherever I go. The amazing thing is that this is true for all of us. When we start to view the world as a friendly place that nurtures and supports us, the universe opens up to us and the possibilities are endless.

Goal: Be open to making new friends today.

December 13

If things were easy to find,
they wouldn't be worth finding.

——*Extremely Loud and Incredibly Close*

I feel blessed that I've pretty much always known what I wanted to do with my life. But I know plenty of people who are still figuring out what that means to them. As long as you stay open and keep following your dreams—even if they feel underdeveloped—you will find that place within yourself.

Goal: Are you doing what you've always wanted to do? If you're not, there's no time like the present—start this moment.

December 14

Always forgive your enemies; nothing annoys them so much.

——OSCAR WILDE

Forgiveness can seem so hard, especially when you are really hurt by someone else. But when you forgive someone else, you're being the bigger person. When you spend time obsessing over something someone has done to you, it becomes toxic to dwell on their wrongs when they've probably forgotten. Kill them with kindness. When you forgive someone else, you're being the bigger person. When I was being bullied, my mom always told me to turn the other cheek. When I was old enough to understand that phrase, I was able act on it. And it helped me overcome my resentment.

Goal: Forgive someone you're upset with and let go of your resentment.

December 15

Patience is bitter but its fruit is sweet.

—JEAN-JACQUES ROUSSEAU

Having patience in life can be so hard, whether it's with people in your life or if you want something in life badly but you've been waiting for it so long. Sometimes people have to wait years or even longer before they get what they've been working toward. Trust that things will come to you when they are meant to and know that when you have truly been patient the rewards will be better than you could have imagined.

Goal: Be patient with those around you, your dreams, and above all—yourself.

December 16

Violence only leads to more violence.
We must all be peaceful warriors.

Violence is an endless cycle. It's so much easier to fight fire with fire but it's futile, a useless venture. It takes so much more energy, thought, creativity, and courage to stand up and be willing to engage in a conversation with someone who doesn't agree with you. You can still come to a place of tolerance and respect without agreeing. We all have to be willing to communicate and respect one another even when we disagree.

Goal: Resist violence and demand respect and open communication. Be willing to see something a different way. Be willing to see the other person's side.

December 17

You will not be punished for your anger,
you will be punished by your anger.

——BUDDHA

Anger and resentment are two of the most toxic emotions we can feel. There are always times when people infuriate us or hurt our feelings but we don't confront it. Instead we just let these negative feelings grow wild within us. Before we know it, they have taken over us like vines crawling over every cell and organ in our body. We should never let someone else's problems bring us down in the first place.

Goal: When someone does something that upsets you, don't hold a grudge; confront them and then do your best to put it behind you.

December 18

Take me by the hand, let's compromise.

—THE FORMAT, "THE COMPROMISE"

Relationships involve two people, which means that just your opinions and ideas aren't enough for a relationship to work. You have to make room for the other person to express themselves as well. It doesn't mean you have to agree on everything because you won't and that's fine. But if you can't find a middle ground and a compromise then you will find yourself alone.

Goal: Work together with friends, family, or coworkers to find compromises when you hit roadblocks.

Do what you can, with what you have, where you are.

—THEODORE ROOSEVELT

We all deserve respect and to know where we stand. But I have so many girlfriends who put up with guys who don't treat them the way they deserve. These guys make promises they can't deliver and are misleading about their real intentions. A friend of mine was dating a guy for over a month, and from the beginning she told him she really liked him and wanted a boyfriend, not just a casual hookup. But he never committed to her; he kept the lines so blurry. She kept saying that she believed she could change him, and convince him to love her if they spent a little more time together. Of course she never changed him. He showed his true colors right away but she ignored the signs because she hoped for more.

Goal: When someone won't or can't commit to something, don't force it. Accept it or walk away.

December 20

Let go and let God.

—ANONYMOUS

When you are struggling with something greater than yourself and all else fails, you just have to be willing to hand your problems over to something greater than yourself. Whether you believe in God, Allah, or the power of the universe, each of us has a higher power within and around us. Just realizing and accepting that you're not in control of everything in this life is actually very liberating and can lead to powerful things.

Goal: Think of those things you're holding on to, breathe, and hand them over to your higher power.

December 21

Your phone doesn't have the answer to your happiness—you do.

Each one of us spends so much time on our cell phones that they might as well be glued to our bodies. I'm not criticizing because I often have the same problem, but recently I have started resisting reaching for my phone. I find I'm using it as a distraction to ignore my thoughts when I should be embracing them.

Goal: Put down your phone today. When you have the urge to play games or look at photos or old text messages, take a deep breath and find something or someone beautiful around you to admire.

December 22

Procrastination is like a credit card: it's a lot of fun until you get the bill.

—CHRISTOPHER PARKER

Everyone knows that they're not supposed to procrastinate but we all do it every now and again. The more things you put off, the more will build up and you will just feel out of control and stressed.

Goal: Manage and prioritize your time and tasks.

December 23

Faith does not exist without doubt.

——UNKNOWN

I heard my pastor say this at a sermon and I was so moved by the message and beauty of this phrase. Every one of us has moments of doubt where we question why we're here and whether or not we're doing the right thing. It's okay to question your journey because it means that you care and are thoughtful. If you didn't have doubts then there wouldn't be anything to have faith in.

Goal: Acknowledge your doubts and do some deep thinking over why you feel that way.

December 24

Think abundantly and you will
receive abundance.

Allow yourself to think about every single thing you want your life to be. If something comes into your head and you think it's too much or that you can't have it then allow that thought to float away as quickly as it came.

Goal: Make a list of your wishes, resolutions, and hopes for next year.

December 25

Family gives us strength and builds our character.

Everything I have gone through I could not have done without the love, faith, and support of my family. Just being around them brings me joy and I forget about any problem or fear I have. They accept me with all of my flaws, and I accept them as well, no matter what.

Goal: Soak up the love of your family today. Love them for everything they are and aren't.

December 26

It does not matter how slow you go, only that you do not stop.

—CONFUCIUS

Speed is relative. Some people move quickly and others move slow. It doesn't mean you are getting more done either way; all that matters is you keep going. No matter what.

Goal: Go at a slower pace today, starting with the moment you open your eyes till the moment you close them and everything in between.

December 27

Stay strong.

Each one of us struggles with something in this life. I realized that no matter where I am, there is a bigger purpose; I use my voice and inspire people, help people get through their problems, and help pick people up when they're down. I am only able to get through each day because of my fans, who inspire me to do what I do and inspire me to stay strong each and every day.

Goal: Stay strong for yourself, and if you have it in you, find the strength to stay strong for someone else.

December 28

When your problems are bigger than you, it's important to reach out for help.

Sometimes we feel overwhelmed and even ashamed by our problems. Before I started treatment for bulimia and cutting, I was hiding from everyone, myself included. I was scared to ask for help and felt so deeply embarrassed about what I was doing I thought it would never end. If you or someone you know is suffering or struggling with any issue, it is so important to get help. You could be saving your life or the life of someone you love.

Goal: Don't hide from yourself or others. Seek help.

December 29

The nice thing about rain is that
it always stops. Eventually.

——EEYORE

Hard times are unavoidable. They pop up when we least expect it—when we're just not ready. But it's important to take comfort in the fact that it can't and won't go on forever.

Goal: As you forge ahead, remind yourself that you're only getting stronger with each challenge you are presented with.

December 30

Man, when you lose your laugh, you lose your footing.

—KEN KESEY

There will be times when we feel knocked down at every turn. Grief, depression, breakups, and so much more. It's important to preserve a sense of humor. You have to remember to laugh at these things or they'll control you. Laughter will help you see the light in the darkest of times. It's more powerful than you'll ever know.

Goal: Even at your lowest points, keep your sense of humor and use it.

December 31

And now we welcome the new year,
full of things that have never been.

—RAINER MARIA RILKE

Spend some time reassessing the past year. Think about how you have grown, how you've changed, what you'd like to continue doing, and what you're ready to move on from. I always find the last few days of the year are packed with so much intense energy and possibility for change that the best thing you can do is sit and reflect.

Goal: Make a list of all that you've accomplished this year.

Acknowledgments

Thank you to everyone at CAST Recovery, Philymack, Inc., Derris and Company, Macmillan, CAA, Hertz, Lichtenstein & Young, the Nordlinger Group, and everyone else on my team. Special thanks to Anna Roberto, Jean Feiwel, and Rachel Fleischer. Much love and thanks for the support of my wonderful friends and family . . . you know who you are!

Resources

Help and support is available from many organizations and treatment centers, but here are two that I recommend:

The Meadows treatment center in Wickenburg, Arizona, is one of the nation's premier programs for treating addiction and psychological trauma, through the Meadows Model, 12-step practices, and the holistic healing of mind, body, and spirit. www.themeadows.com

CAST Recovery offers a range of services and treatment/therapy. Demi Lovato has partnered with CAST Recovery to create the Lovato Treatment Scholarship to cover expenses for someone struggling with mental health and/or addiction issues. www.castrecovery.com